PORTRAIT OF THE
Terriers

Handel Kardas

Ian Allan
PUBLISHING

Acknowledgements

My thanks are due to those who have helped me in preparing this book. The assistance of Mike Esau, Klaus Marx, Brian Morrison, Dick Riley and others, who have generously allowed access to their photographic collections and permitted some plundering of the same, is particularly appreciated. Grateful thanks to Colin Binnie for permission to reproduce his 'Terrier' drawings from *The Brighton Terriers*. I am grateful to the active preservationists who have contributed in various ways, especially those who found time to 'talk Terriers' and made Chapter 7 possible. As always, I acknowledge the work of previous authors, whose books or articles I have referred to and whose past efforts have made mine that much easier. I must pay tribute to Bradley and Campbell Cornwell in particular, for their masterly definitive works. Finally, my thanks to those who have seen and commented on the text as it took shape — their advice has helped me to avoid all sorts of pitfalls.

First published 1999

ISBN 0 7110 2652 1

Published by Ian Allan Publishing

an imprint of Ian Allan Publishing Ltd, Terminal House, Shepperton, Surrey TW17 8AS. Printed by Ian Allan Printing Ltd, Riverdene Business Park, Hersham, Surrey KT12 4RG.

Code: 9906/B

Publisher's note: In a number of instances buffers and chimneys were already cropped from the original prints. We wish to apologise should this spoil your enjoyment of this book.

Front cover:
Stepney, preserved on the Bluebell Railway, heads towards Horsted Keynes on 27 October 1983.
Mike Esau

Back cover, top:
Sutton, wearing Kent & East Sussex Railway livery is seen behind BR-liveried *Poplar* on 13 October 1985. The latter was an original KESR locomotive — No 3 *Bodiam*. *Mike Esau*

Back cover, bottom:
A driver's eye-view from the footplate of *Stepney* on the Bluebell Railway.
R. C. Riley

Title page:
Last day of BR passenger service for the class, 2 November 1963. *Whitechapel* passes photographers as it leaves Havant for Hayling Island.
Mike Esau

Above:
Gipsyhill in the early 1880s. This loco ended its active career as a member of the Great Western Railway's capital stock. *Locomotive Publishing Co/ Ian Allan Library*

Below:
Tooting on the turntable at Eastbourne shed in the 1880s. *Locomotive Publishing Co/ Ian Allan Library*

Contents

Bibliography

In the course of their long careers, 'Terriers' have been the subjects of many published works. Those listed here are the ones principally referred to.

Bradley, D. L.: *The Locomotives of the London Brighton & South Coast Railway Part 1*; Railway Correspondence & Travel Society, 1969.

Bradley, D. L.: *A Locomotive History of Railways on the Isle of Wight*; Railway Correspondence & Travel Society, 1982.

Campbell Cornwell, H. J.: *William Stroudley, Craftsman of Steam*; David & Charles, 1968.

Cooper, Peter: *LBSCR Stock Book*; Runpast Publishing, 1990.

Hamilton Ellis, C.: *The London Brighton & South Coast Railway*; Ian Allan, 1960.

Marx, Klaus: *Famous Fenchurch*; Bluebell Railway Preservation Society, 1972.

Marx, Klaus: *I'm Stepney*; Bluebell Railway Preservation Society, 1982.

Middlemass, Tom: *Stroudley and his 'Terriers'*; Pendragon Partnership, 1995.

Periodicals

Railway Magazine (IPC), *Railway World* (Ian Allan) and the now-defunct *Locomotive* have all carried articles and news reports on 'Terriers' over many years. Other sources consulted include the Stephenson Locomotive Society's *Journal* and the RCTS's *Railway Observer*. The Society magazines *Bluebell News*, *Tenterden Terrier* and *Wight Report* (now *Island Rail News*) are valuable sources of information in respect of the preserved 'Terriers'.

Below:
Sutton at Eastleigh in its final BR condition.
Ian Allan Library

Foreword

To attempt to do justice to the remarkable 'Terrier' tanks within a book of reasonable size has proved to be an interesting challenge. There is so much that could be said; they are Britain's oldest surviving class of steam engines in any quantity; they belong to the beginnings of modern locomotive design, coming from that Victorian leap forward in railway technology. Placed alongside engines designed many years later, they are recognisably of the same school of thought although older (and smaller), while earlier machines had an archaic quality which clearly labelled them as belonging to a previous era.

That there are 10 survivors, seven of which can be counted as active in preservation, is remarkable. Not surprisingly there have been other books written on the class and they have featured in other works too, including many magazine articles over the past 120-odd years.

Below:
The preserved *Sutton* (originally *Whitechapel*) descends Tenterden Bank on the Kent & East Sussex Railway with a demonstration mixed train in the early 1980s. *Mike Esau*

I have therefore been following well-trodden ground. Rather than repeating what has been done, especially various blow-by-blow accounts where the simple facts of the 'Terrier' story can still be read, I have aimed to put the engines into their proper context, the ever-developing world of the railways, in which they were a small but significant constant for a surprisingly long time — a point which itself needs explaining. I have also given what I believe to be due prominence to the last 35 or so years, in which the active survivors have played a useful part in our heritage railway scene, for I believe that it would be quite wrong, as some do, to consider that history stopped at the time of entry into preservation. Likewise, our heritage railways are effectively the only places where people with first-hand experience of working with 'Terriers' can now be found. A few of those concerned have helped bring this book to life in a way that descriptions of the past never could.

One of the curiosities of the 'Terrier' story is that locomotive men used their names long after these had been removed, in some cases for half a century or more, at sheds where ex-Brighton men remained and kept some of the old traditions alive. I have followed suit here, and referred to the engines by their names. It is not just sentiment, for to use numbers is more confusing when nearly all were renumbered at least once and some carried five different numbers in their long lives. Relatively few (mainly the Isle of Wight engines) were renamed and in their cases I have used the name which makes best sense in the context. It will, I hope, make it easier to follow the sometimes convoluted history of the class.

Finally, when the 'Terriers' first appeared, the hobby of photography was barely a decade old. Images of 'Terriers' in their early days are relatively few, normally of static engines and not of the quality that was to develop later. Inevitably, many have been published before. I hope that their historic significance and the limited scope of alternatives will be an acceptable excuse for including them.

HSK
January 1999

Introduction

There has always been something rather special about the 'Terrier' tanks. The first major class designed by William Stroudley, one of the greatest and most respected of Victorian steam locomotive engineers, they served the London, Brighton & South Coast Railway well for half a century. Though their numbers were gradually diminishing from the original 50, they then worked for its successors, the Southern Railway and British Railways, for another 40 years. The last 10 were not withdrawn until 1963, by which time they were the oldest engines in service on BR and the final elimination of steam traction was only five years away.

Their popularity with the public, railway staff and enthusiasts was due to far more than their long lives. The 'Terriers' had style. Early examples of the modern British locomotive, they long had a reputation, thanks to the excellence and good balance of the design, for doing more work than their small size would suggest. In their original, elaborate livery, the main colour of which was yellow ochre, they were an eye-catching sight on their primary duties on the suburban lines of mid-Victorian South and East London. In later years,

when they had largely fled to rural lines, their neat and balanced design made them attractive in most of the various liveries they carried. They were eye-catching machines and they caught the public imagination as few classes of steam engine have done.

Given that their career was remarkably long, it is not surprising that 10 have survived; three in museums and seven on preserved railways, where they are highly regarded as active members of the locomotive fleets. No other class of Victorian locomotive has survived in anything like such numbers and their surviving contemporaries are nearly all confined to museums with appearances in steam severely limited, if permitted at all.

Nearly 130 years after they were introduced, the surviving 'Terriers' have acquired individual variations in the course of their many overhauls, repairs and full rebuilds. Most of the key stages of 'Terrier' history can still be seen and, with some of the developments going on to keep the class at work, it is likely that other stages will be seen again in the future.

The 'Terriers' owe their long career to three things — a good design, versatility and popularity. It is likely that these factors will keep them active for many years to come, to the delight of new generations of passengers and enthusiasts. In charting an almost unique locomotive history in this book, one of the best bits is being able to say that it is not over yet.

Below:
The first 'Terrier' to enter active preservation, *Stepney* is seen at Sheffield Park, Bluebell Railway, newly repainted into a close approximation of Stroudley livery (adapted to fit its 'A1X' status) in 1961.
Ian Allan Library/Madgwick Collection

CHAPTER ONE

The Hour, the Man — and the Engines

At the end of the 1860s, the London, Brighton & South Coast Railway was not in a happy state. It had weathered the recession that had hit the country hard early in the decade and had seen the end of a number of railway projects but it had not come through undamaged.

The 'Brighton' was a company that depended more on passenger than freight revenue and passenger journeys had fallen. Not only that, but a number of projects for new lines (either associated with or sponsored by the company) had failed, taking a fair bit of capital with them. The company had in fact sailed closer to bankruptcy than it liked to admit. Now, though, its fortunes were improving again, the result of a strong, experienced and cautious management team being put in charge, plus, of course, the increased flow of business. It was this which was bringing to a head a crisis which the bad years had both caused and partly concealed. The company's Locomotive Department was in a mess.

To trim expenses, there had been several years of minimal maintenance. Spare engines had been laid aside. Now they were needed again but were simply not available, as the company's main works at Brighton struggled to cope with the backlog. This was one part of the problem. The other part was the head of the department himself, the Locomotive, Carriage & Wagon Superintendent John Chester Craven.

Craven was a fine engineer and a good administrator who had served the company well and was, on the whole, held in good regard. Early in his tenure, some 20 years before, he had led the development of the company's workshops at Brighton and during the years when the company matured and expanded, had provided it with a

fleet of locomotives to meet its needs and a carriage fleet to meet its budget. He had blind spots though: one seems to have been a belief that once opened, Brighton Works could not be improved; another was his determination to design engines for a specific job. Thus the rapid technological development in the railway industry of the 1850s and 1860s had little effect on Brighton. By 1869 the Works was outdated, expensive to operate — and verging on the chaotic. On the line, the locomotive stock of over 200 was divided into over 70 classes, and so many locos had received 'one-off' modifications that within a class there were few matching machines. Craven's policy, the absolute opposite of standardisation, forced up costs and caused difficulties whenever a substitute loco was required. It could not go on; the company's recovery was being hamstrung. Craven took the view that given time, the problems would resolve themselves. The directors disagreed. They leaned on Craven. When this had little effect, they leaned much harder. Unofficially but firmly, he was

Right:
The man himself; William Stroudley, complete with his 'trademark' umbrella, beside *Brighton* after that engine had won a gold medal at the Paris Exhibition. Handwriting experts will note that his signature bears more than a passing resemblance to F. W. Webb's — indicative, perhaps, of some temperamental similarities? *Ian Allan Library*

Above:
One of the Lochgorm tanks, design forerunners of the 'Terriers'. *R. C. Riley Collection*

advised to consider resigning. In November 1869 he duly gave the company three months' notice. Choosing the right man to replace him has been described as one of the most crucial decisions that the Brighton's Board ever had to make.

The New Superintendent

William Stroudley's background was typical of the second generation of leading railway locomotive engineers. Born in 1833, he had a basic formal education and had started work before his 10th birthday. Having a mechanical aptitude, the crucial move was when he was apprenticed to a Birmingham engineering company aged 15. He climbed rapidly through the ranks of the profession; in 1853 he joined the Great Western as a fitter at Swindon; by 1856 he was foreman fitter at the Great Northern's Peterborough shed; from there he went, in 1861, to be Works Manager at the Edinburgh & Glasgow's Cowlairs Works.

The Stroudley approach began to become apparent. His first priority at Cowlairs was to improve the plant and workshop arrangements. After several years of playing 'second fiddle', he applied for, and got, the post of Locomotive and Carriage Superintendent on the Highland Railway in 1865. Aged just 32 he had reached the top level of the railway engineering profession, albeit on a small company in a bit of a backwater.

Again, his first task was to reorganise

Lochgorm Works. Once that was complete he turned his attention to improving the railway's stock but the tight budget of a struggling company gave him little scope. He improved, rather than replaced, the existing fleet. One highly significant project was the building of a small 0-6-0 tank engine. His talents were obvious: a good organiser, a sound engineer, inventive, willing to be innovative if the innovation was sound, and clearly capable of running a Locomotive Department. Obviously he felt that the Highland Railway offered little scope for his ambitions, for he applied for the Brighton post. The company spies were out and were obviously impressed, for he was on a shortlist of two applicants who were interviewed. He was offered and accepted the post at the end of December, taking up his duties on 1 February 1870. The LBSC was about to experience a revolution.

Below:
The Brighton Works erecting shop, apparently in the 1900s. Nearly every visible locomotive is a Stroudley. *Ian Allan Library/Madgwick Collection*

Above:
The earliest known photograph of a 'Terrier'.
Fenchurch is posed for its official photograph outside
the Works paint shop, newly finished and ready to
enter service. It is fitted with plain three-link couplings
and the condensing pipe linking the tanks is evident
just in front of the cab. *R. C. Riley Collection*

Above left:
Brighton Works in 1870. In the background the London
Road Viaduct and the line to Lewes cross open fields.
Ian Allan Library/Madgwick Collection

Left:
Brighton Running Shed and the Works beyond, in the
early 1890s, with evidence in the background of how
the town's population had grown since 1870. On shed,
every loco except that on the extreme left is a
Stroudley machine.
Ian Allan Library/Madgwick Collection

The Birth of Two Legends

Stroudley was now in charge of the Locomotive
Department of one of the country's 'top 20'
railway companies. The company was compact;
its system was roughly contained in a triangle
formed by London, Portsmouth and Hastings. Its
London suburban network was still growing and
new lines were planned in the country areas. It
was relatively small and its locomotive fleet was
numbered in hundreds rather than the thousands
of the London & North Western, the biggest of
them all. Curiously, Stroudley was an almost exact
contemporary of F. W. Webb, who was shortly to
take command at Crewe. But while Webb ran his
huge empire with a psychological reign of terror
(and for a while almost ran the town of Crewe
itself), Stroudley's style was most suited to a
smaller outfit. He was the visible and known
leader, familiar to the whole department — and it
worked. There arose on the Brighton a sort of
Stroudley Cult, which lasted long after his death.
That is not to say he was not a typical Victorian
manager; he was as much a martinet as Webb
when the need arose, and the banging of his
umbrella tip on the ground was an indication of
disapproval known and feared at every workshop
and running shed on the line.

He was stocky, short-sighted and asthmatic,
strong-minded with a magnetic personality and a
humane approach. He was soon winning the
support of the men in a department whose
morale had suffered badly, while he assessed
what the Brighton needed.

Once again, he saw as his first task the reorganisation of Brighton Works. Little trace of this workshop complex, where the 'Terriers' and many other classes were to be built over the next 80 years, now remains. Anyone who has known Brighton station only in the last 30 years might not realise that the large car park perched on the hillside to the east and north of the station, stands on the site of the old locomotive works. Only the fragments on the west of the main line, long adapted for multiple-unit use, now remain. Stroudley spent two years and a great deal of money reducing the Craven chaos to order, rebuilding and re-equipping. The LBSC Board, having chosen their man, bit the bullet, supported his plans and found the cash. Little was done to the locomotive fleet in this time, beyond maintenance and a start on removing some of the worst anomalies. But by early 1872 Stroudley felt able to start on the strategic development of the fleet and he soon turned to where the problem was greatest: the London inner suburban lines. It was for these lines that the 'Terriers' were built.

There were two lines in particular that were suffering from the inadequacies of ageing Craven machinery; the South London and East London lines. The East London, running north from New Cross, through Brunel's Thames Tunnel, traversing the docklands to meet with the North Thames systems at Shoreditch, was more a freight than a passenger line and undeniably went through some of the grimmest parts of the East End. The South London line was rather smarter, though these days that suggestion would raise eyebrows in some quarters! It linked London Bridge with Victoria by way of Peckham Rye, Denmark Hill, Clapham and Battersea Park. Opened in the mid-1860s, when the need for economy had been a vital factor, it was lightly-laid, with shallow ballast and light iron rails. The gradient profile was like a saw blade, with the worst of all — the 1 in 64 Grosvenor Road Bank — hitting trains just as they were getting away from Victoria. A little over nine miles long, the line had 11 intermediate stations. The line's main business was workers going to and from the City and West End, with heavy morning and early evening traffic and far less for the rest of the day. The line was not attracting the traffic that it should — something had to be done to make it more tempting to potential passengers. Equally, from the operating point of view, it needed to be worked more smartly, reliably and cheaply.

Stroudley's analysis was that a small but relatively powerful tank engine was needed, to meet the constraints of light axle-load, a quick turn-round at termini, snappy acceleration and a reasonable running speed. His first proposal looked remarkably like the Lochgorm tank but smaller, an 0-6-0T with a domeless boiler, weighing only about 20 tons. This was drawn out in mid-1871 but Stroudley was soon having second thoughts, perhaps as the result of a few footplate trips on the South London line. More power, to have something in reserve for the twice-daily peaks, more weight for better adhesion, and a boiler with a dome — obviously he decided that the frequent starting and stopping on changing gradients would set up boiler water surges that could get water carried into the cylinders if there was no dome to act as a steam collector.

By early 1872 the engines as they were to appear were largely drawn out, although the dome was quite a late addition. By midsummer work was well in hand on the first batch of six. On 9 September No 72 *Fenchurch* was the first of the class to enter service, at Battersea Shed, and a locomotive legend was born.

Right:
A mid-1870s view of *Wapping* in service. The early coupling has been replaced by a screw coupling and the wooden brake blocks show considerable wear compared with the new ones seen on *Fenchurch*. The picture also shows a 'Terrier' characteristic: the buffer castings stand proud of the footplate, a consequence of the low footplate height and shallow buffer beam.
R. C. Riley Collection

Dates of entry to service (listed by batch)

1.

70	*Poplar*	November 1872
71	*Wapping*	September 1872
72	*Fenchurch*	September 1872
73	*Deptford*	October 1872
74	*Shadwell*	October 1872
75	*Blackwall*	October 1872

2.

64	*Kemptown*	June 1874
65	*Tooting*	June 1874
66	*Hatcham*	June 1874
67	*Brixton*	June 1874
68	*Clapham*	August 1874
69	*Peckham*	August 1874

3.

58	*Wandle*	October 1875
59	*Cheam*	October 1875
60	*Ewell*	October 1875
61	*Sutton*	October 1875

NB — each batch shown in numerical order rather than chronological

62	*Martello*	October 1875
63	*Preston*	October 1875
52	*Surrey*	December 1875
53	*Ashtead*	December 1875
54	*Waddon*	December 1875
55	*Stepney*	December 1875
56	*Shoreditch*	November 1875
57	*Thames*	November 1875

4.

46	*Newington*	December 1876
47	*Cheapside*	December 1876
48	*Leadenhall*	December 1876
49	*Bishopsgate*	December 1876
50	*Whitechapel*	December 1876
51	*Rotherhithe*	December 1876

5.

41	*Piccadilly*	June 1877
42	*Tulsehill*	June 1877
43	*Gipsyhill*	June 1877

44	*Fulham*	June 1877
45	*Merton*	June 1877
76	*Hailsham*	June 1877

6.

35	*Morden*	June 1878
36	*Bramley*	June 1878
37	*Southdown*	May 1878
38	*Millwall*	May 1878
39	*Denmark*	May 1878
40	*Brighton*	March 1878

7.

77	*Wonersh*	June 1880
78	*Knowle*	June 1880
79	*Minories*	June 1880
80	*Bookham*	June 1880
81	*Beulah*	July 1880
82	*Boxhill*	July 1880
83	*Earlswood*	August 1880
84	*Crowborough*	September 1880

CHAPTER TWO

At Home in London — and Beyond

To say that a class was an immediate success is a dangerous cliché (overworked and too often an exaggeration) but in the case of the 'Terriers' it is true. By the end of 1872 all that first batch of six were at work and things were looking up on the South London line. More to the point with hindsight, they had captured the enthusiastic approval of their crews, an approval which was to develop into affection; they had caught the attention of the railway press; and they were being noticed by the public.

There were several reasons for this remarkable success of such small engines. They were just right for the job, thanks to Stroudley's

engineering skill and his ability to read the situation correctly, and they reflected his artistic streak and his flair for marketing.

Taking the technical side of the 'Terriers' first, the design was masterful. The boiler, though small, was very free-steaming and surprisingly economical. Its use of coal was almost miserly. A 'Terrier' could do a day's work on the South London line for an average fuel consumption of less than 24lb per mile, including the coal used in lighting up at the start of the day. This was well under what the Craven engines used and for years was about two-thirds of what the South Eastern Railway could manage on its suburban services.

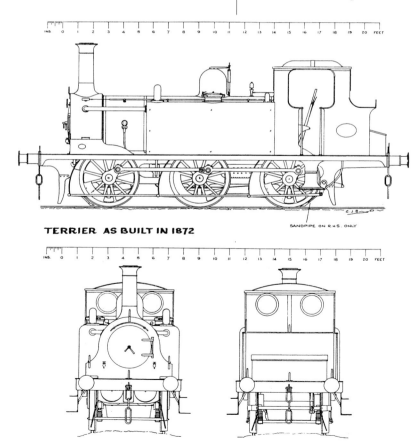

TERRIER AS BUILT IN 1872

SANDPIPE ON R.H.S. ONLY

The LBSC accountants and the firemen of Battersea and New Cross sheds were won over on the spot.[1]

It was just as well for the firemen that the engines were so economical to fire, for once under way on the South London's distinctly iffy track, they bounced around so much that getting the coal into the right place was more a matter of luck than skill. But a 'Terrier' was happy with a few shovelfuls round the box at each station stop and a fire made up well at the terminus, so firing on the move was rarely a problem.

Filling the boiler was also made simpler, by the provision of pumps rather than injectors. Injector technology was still comparatively new and the designs available could be troublesome on rough track. They also played up like anything when expected to feed hot water, which was why Stroudley used pumps instead. Like all his designs for the Brighton, the 'Terriers' were fitted with condensing apparatus as an economy measure. Part of the exhaust steam from the cylinders was diverted before passing through the blastpipe, going instead to the water tanks. It fanned across the water surface of the left-hand tank then went through a link pipe into the right-hand tank, by when most of it had condensed back into the feed water. Any remaining returned to the smokebox and escaped to the atmosphere via the chimney. The result was that the feed water soon heated up and could approach boiling point in favourable conditions. No injector would touch such hot water; Stroudley's design of pumps took it in their stride.

Condensing gave a double advantage. Hot feed water gave a small but significant increase in the locomotive's thermal efficiency (a saving of just two or three percent was important when you measured coal consumption in trainloads per day) and it led to a slight reduction in the need for feed water — and it is often overlooked that supplying locomotives with water costs money. There was, unfortunately, a disadvantage to Stroudley's system. The tanks could overfill as a result of condensation and there was then a risk of water splashing through the steam return pipe, giving the smokebox interior a quick wash down and blowing out of the chimney in a black, smutty shower. The Victorian travelling public were less than impressed if this shower caught them when a train ran into a station braking hard, when the calamity was most likely to happen, and were vociferous in their complaints. Presumably the LBSC took the view that the solution was a matter of good enginemanship, for the condensers remained in place until the 1890s, when Billinton, Stroudley's successor, began removing them, only for Marsh, the next chief, to put them back when economy again became paramount!

From the driver's point of view, he had a well-designed cab to work in, with the controls well

[1] Years later the railway journalist Ahrons, describing a volcanic and deafening footplate ride on a Webb compound in full cry, declared that a 'Terrier' would have been able to run on what it threw up the chimney

positioned for convenience. If there was a fault, it was that the regulator was rather stiff to operate, a result of the simple design. But he had a good view, whether running forwards or in reverse, all the steam he needed unless his fireman was a severe incompetent, and best of all perhaps, he had his name painted in the cab, a reminder to all concerned that this was his engine. Unsurprisingly, many a driver became fiercely protective, and if his baby was not turned out immaculately by the shed cleaning gangs, somebody would catch it hot and strong!

Comparatively large cylinders for driving wheels of just 4ft diameter gave a snappy acceleration and a good turn of speed, which was what was needed on the South London. Braking was less well provided at first. The importance of stopping a train as smartly as starting it had not yet fully penetrated railway culture. Large wooden brake blocks were actuated by a handwheel, which worked well enough, or by steam, which worked too well.

Above:
Bunker, toolbox and livery detail. (*Stepney*, 1998.)
Author

Below:
Detail of front buffer, showing the elaborate lining-out. Note the shed-code painted on the valance plate.
S. C. Townroe

Above:
Cabside numberplate; *Stepney's* replica of the original.
Author

Below:
Cab front and whistle detail. *S. C. Townroe*

Above:
Name lettering detail, on *Stepney*, 1998. *Author*

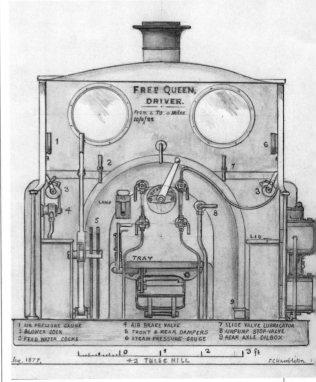

Top left:
Rear view of *Hailsham* showing bunker and tool-box arrangement. Large lumps of coal, while making it easier to stack the small bunker high with fuel, made extra work for the fireman when they reached the shovelling stage! *Ian Allan Library/Madgwick Collection*

Top right:
Its smart appearance slightly marred by a bucket slung on the tank top, *Fulham* is seen at Brighton station. Presumably it is doing a stint of pilot duties at its home shed, running coal wagons into the coaling stage. Squeezed into the 'vee' between the London and East Coast lines, many movements on Brighton Shed involved dropping into the ends of the platform roads. *O. J. Morris/Madgwick Collection*

Above:
Back from the 1878 Paris Exhibition, *Brighton* had her achievement painted above the name — a proud addition to an already immaculate engine. Stroudley showed something of a soft spot for *Brighton* — it was used several times as a mobile test-bed for new ideas. *Ian Allan Library*

Right:
Cab and backhead section drawing of *Tulsehill*, showing the simple but convenient layout of the controls. *F. C. Hambleton/R. C. Riley Collection*

Steam stops were harsh and there was a risk of locking the loco's wheels and wearing flats on them, which was a sure recipe for a first class rocket when authority found out. So on the engine the fireman diligently wound on the handbrake while at the back of the train the guard frantically did the same and between them they managed to stop the train in the right place on most occasions. The fully-fitted train equipped with the Westinghouse air brake was a boon and a blessing when it arrived on the LBSC a few years later (strongly recommended by Stroudley) and nowhere more so than on the South London, where it meant you could run fast enough to meet the schedule with no nagging doubt about being able to stop at the next station.[2]

The Traffic Department was delighted that at last it could run the South London reliably and

[2]*Stroudley adopted the Westinghouse air brake because evidence showed that it was the best available. At Crewe, it is said, Webb threw George Westinghouse off the premises after the latter made the terrible faux pas of attempting to bribe him, and eventually adopted the vacuum brake instead; the incident was to delay the universal adoption of the air brake by almost a century.*

was even more pleased when complementary sets of carriages, also designed by Stroudley, began to arrive. These four-wheeled coaches were ideal for the job of moving lots of people, if questionable in other respects. A vehicle seating 50 passengers weighed little over six tons. Compare that with a modern suburban coach, weighing around 30 tons and carrying about 100, many of whom will be standing, and it is clear that rolling stock design has advanced a great deal in most ways, if not in all. Certainly the low weight was achieved largely by building almost flimsy bodies, and it is just as well that there was never a serious collision on the line in steam days. Safety aside, this stock meant that a 'Terrier' could work a 10- or 12-coach train with ease, shifting some 500 passengers at a time in the rush hours, while the dead weight of a shortened train was not too critical when costed against the lighter loads of midday and evenings.

The excellent combination of effective boiler and powerful 'works' was all held together by a surprisingly light set of frames. To save weight the frame plates were as shallow as possible and further lightened by big slots cut between the axleboxes. Even today, the impression given by a

Right:
The Rooter Roundhouse at New Cross, the home of the depot's 'Terriers' for many years. Due to its small size it was largely unused once the class had left New Cross and when photographed in 1938 was getting rather ruinous. The Blitz was soon to complete its demise. *R. C. Riley*

Right:
When larger engines began replacing 'Terriers' from London, *Bookham* was transferred to Littlehampton. It is seen here with the Craven 0-4-2ST *Bognor*, which was replaced on the Barnham-Bognor branch duties by *Millwall* at about the same time. *LGRP*

Above:
Above:
In Billinton condition, *Poplar* stands at Selsdon Road with the Woodside line train, comprising three Stroudley four-wheelers. Photographers of the day (official or otherwise) needed so long to set up their cameras that staff had ample time to observe them and strike attitudes! *R. C. Riley Collection*

'Terrier' under the footplate is that there is not much holding it all together; but it is clearly adequate, for it has been doing so for over 125 years in some cases. The whole locomotive weighed a little under 25 tons in working order and the weight was distributed so well that in theory each axle carried the same — an almost ideal arrangement, especially for an engine likely to work equally forwards and backwards.

The overall aesthetics of the design were as good as its engineering. So good that for all its small size, a 'Terrier' was immediately eye-catching and — just as important — pleasing to most eyes. Part of the secret of the class's undoubted popularity with the public, as well as enthusiasts, throughout its life is that the engines are nice to look at. Despite being compact and noticeably small, especially when coupled to coaches, a 'Terrier' is very well proportioned. The small wheels fit its length well and the footplate, lower than is usual, looks just right above them. The boiler is quite low-slung, with side-tanks in proportion. At its ends a neat cab and a tall chimney rise in a sort of counterpoint. Roughly central between them, the dome is capped with Salter safety valves, whose spring balance arms run backwards to the tops of polished brass spring-housings that drop back to the boiler top.

As first built, the dome was set slightly back

from the boiler mid-point and the short smokebox had a front which merged into the fronts of the sandboxes on the leading wheel splashers. This front wingplate styling gave a series of graceful curves, which were lost when the class were rebuilt with longer smokeboxes in the 20th century. Likewise, the Stroudley chimney with its polished copper trim at the top, was replaced with a cast-iron chimney. But the end result of these changes, the work of Marsh, was still a nicely balanced design that lost little of its charm.

The cab was adorned front and back with a pair of large spectacle windows; round and with brightly polished brass frames, they gave a vaguely humanoid look to the engine. The cab roof, too, was unusual, for instead of being curved in an arc, it was flat round the edges and dished upwards in the middle: a definite Stroudleyism, designed to cut down on noise by reducing drumming. Behind the cab was a small coal bunker, carrying little more than half a ton, and behind this again was another Stroudley signature piece, a tool box. On the cabside was, before long, the Westinghouse pump, that gave the 'Terriers' (and of course other air-braked engines) one of their station characteristics; standing on a train, the engine would make a 'phoo, phoo' noise from its chimney as the pump beat, rather than the endless roar of a vacuum ejector. Westinghouse-fitted 'Terriers' still do it and it does not take overmuch imagination to compare it with panting for breath; small wonder that children find 'Terriers' more user-friendly than bigger engines.

It is remarkable how little the appearance of the 'Terriers' changed over their 90-ish years of main line service. The main change was the Marsh rebuild already mentioned, that converted them from 'A1' to 'A1X' class: the new boiler included a longer smokebox that saw the end of the wingplates and raised front sandboxes, leaving the smokebox as a cylinder on an exposed saddle, with the sandboxes below the running plate. The substitution of original chimneys by cast-iron ones went on steadily over the years as the originals wore out and the Marsh boiler had the dome set a few inches further forward to nearer the mid-position. Unlike Marsh's reboilerings of other Stroudley classes, the 'Terriers' kept their Salter safety valves — to the benefit of their looks. The only other significant visual change affected those 'Terriers' that worked on the Isle of Wight. Their coal capacity was increased by removing the tool box and extending the bunker backwards, roughly doubling its capacity. The value of this conversion is shown in that no 'Terrier' returning from the island had its original rear end restored, either in Southern Railway, British Railways or preserved line service.

But undoubtedly the icing on the cake, that which really drew public attention to the 'Terriers', was their bright, elaborate livery. Apart from a demonstration on a Craven engine to win

over the directors, the 'Terriers' were the first of the Brighton's famed 'yellow engines'.

To call the colour yellow, though, is to cheapen it and to ignore the detail that made the end result so fetching. It was not its first appearance, for Stroudley had used it on the Highland Railway, but the 'Terriers' were its first manifestation on the LBSC, where it was to be standard until replaced by the equally smart but less showy rich umber in the 1900s.

The colour was a light, bright, yellowy brown, sometimes called yellow ochre, occasionally referred to as Oxford green, Oxford ochre or gamboge. In LBSC language it has long been 'improved engine green', which is supposed to be the name Stroudley gave it and is sometimes taken as evidence that he was colour-blind. However, official references to improved engine green are ambiguous and could just as well refer to the dark ivy green he introduced for goods engines (the Craven livery was Brunswick green for all types), so the case remains unproven either way. These days, the term 'Stroudley yellow' is sometimes used and at least has the virtue of clarity.[3]

The livery's detail produced such a harmonious effect that it seems unlikely that it was the product of a colour-blind man. Outside the main yellow panels was a broad border of dark olive green, separated from the yellow by a black band

Below:
Gipsyhill was transferred to Portsmouth; it is seen here in Billinton condition at Bognor in 1899, at the head of a Barnham train. While *Millwall* was the official Bognor branch engine, it often had the assistance of a second 'Terrier', sometimes sub-shedded at Bognor's rather basic running shed.
Ian Allan Library/Bucknall Collection

[3]*Just to further muddy the issue, in dog-showing circles an almost identical colour is officially 'red'.*

edged with white and red lines. The boiler cleading bands were olive green, similarly picked out. Buffer beams had a bright red centre panel with a claret surround, the two being separated by elaborate bordering. Outer frames were black; the inner frame faces and most of the motion between were red, the connecting rods being left bright. The inner and outer cab roof were white — and they had to stay white. On the side tanks was the name, in large gilt letters, shaded black to the right and blocked in red fading through white to blue on the left. The number was carried on a large, oval, brass plate on the cabside. The whole effect was elaborate in the extreme, and bright, cheerful, even flamboyant. It certainly caught the public's attention, especially for the paradox that these strikingly-painted engines were working through some pretty gloomy, smoke-laden suburbs. How far people identified with the names is open to question, especially as those on the first six — *Poplar*, *Wapping*, *Fenchurch*, *Deptford*, *Shadwell* and *Blackwall* — owed more to East than South London. But the names stuck none the less and one of the extraordinary twists to the 'Terriers'' tale is that, in Brighton territory at least, the engines were still known to loco staff by their names in early BR days, more than 40 years after they had been painted over.

Stroudley, of course, was planning a larger class and must have been delighted when the operating side of the railway began clamouring for more of them as soon as possible. Once he was satisfied that the design was right, and once the sole serious teething trouble had been solved, more did follow: six in mid-1874, 12 in 1875, and so on until the last of the 50 entered traffic in September 1880. All but six of them were based in London, shedded at Battersea or New Cross, where each shed had a roundhouse reserved for its 'Terrier' fleet.[4]

The sole serious teething trouble was the cylinder blocks. All the first six were given new cylinders within a few years, the original design proving troublesome. It was this in fact which

stopped *Poplar* or *Wapping* (numerically the first two) from being the first in traffic. *Wapping's* cylinders were found faulty and condemned before it had even left the erecting shop and it was given the set earmarked for *Poplar*. This changeover held *Wapping* back and pushed poor *Poplar* well down the queue, giving *Fenchurch* the chance to leapfrog to the coveted 'first in traffic' status that still backs its claim to being the oldest of the class and the oldest standard gauge, main line, regularly operating locomotive in Britain.[5]

The LBSC staff and officials were pleased; so were the directors, who had their clearest proof to date that they had chosen the right man for the job. The travelling public were impressed. More broadly, of course, the public took no notice, as the mass media of the day ignored the arrival of the 'Terriers'. They had a fair excuse; unlike its modern successors, the Brighton did not introduce new stock with grand press launches featuring dancing girls, pyrotechnic displays, special runs, souvenir paperweights and large, mainly liquid, lunches, in the hope of a few column inches in *The Times*.

However, the railway technical press did take notice and was impressed. Read by railway professionals and the enthusiasts of the day, such magazines as the *Engineer* had some influence and when they heaped praise on this new suburban class, their opinions were respected.

It is from the *Engineer* that we first learn of the class's nickname. To LBSC officialdom it was Class A; commenting favourably on the class a few months after their appearance, the *Engineer* reported that they were already known as 'Rooters' or 'Terriers' to the staff, being so small, wiry and lively. Anyone who has seen a Jack Russell terrier rushing around enjoying life will appreciate the terrier allusion but 'Rooter' is now less clear and has been the subject of speculation over the years. Was it because they scurried down holes to pass under the Thames, or because they dug in and got on with the job? At any rate, 'Rooter' was the common name among London enginemen while 'Terrier' was more common among enthusiasts, becoming the generally accepted nickname early in the 20th century.

The *Engineer* continued to be generous in its praise in its early 1873 issues:

'...we advise those who have any doubts as to the satisfactory way in which Mr Stroudley conducts his metropolitan traffic...to make a trip from Victoria to London Bridge and back. The *Fenchurch* and *Poplar* are not 'paper' engines but

---

[4]Stroudley's critics have accused him of lack of foresight in building roundhouses suitable only for 'Terriers' at the London depots. But the New Cross building was an old one dating back to the earliest days and at Battersea there were space constraints; a small roundhouse could use an otherwise redundant corner.

[5]As distinct from an industrial locomotive or an occasionally-steamed museum resident.

existing facts and very symmetrical and neat. They look good all over and have been running long enough to prove that they are as good as they look.

'The engines… claim, and are certain to receive, thoughtful attention from every locomotive superintendent who has anything to do with metropolitan traffic. They are in every way worthy of the attention of railway boards and railway engineers, and Mr Stroudley deserves no small credit for the courage and originality which he has shown in putting such engines to work…'

Part of this high praise, no doubt, was due to the editor, Vaughan Pendred, being on friendly terms with Stroudley. After all, what editor would not be friendly with a locomotive superintendent who took the trouble to keep him informed of what was going on and extended a more or less open invitation to come and see for himself whenever he liked? Stroudley's instinct for publicity was paying dividends once again. What a refreshing change he must have been from some other locomotive chiefs, such as James Stirling whose reign on the South Eastern from 1878 to 1898 was marked by a 'shoot on sight' policy towards journalists at Ashford Works, and witch-hunts to find a sackable culprit whenever any SER locomotive department news was leaked to the railway or engineering press. Getting and publishing stories about such railways was a challenge to be savoured, but the friendly and encouraging policies of Stroudley and his like made a warm and sympathetic coverage more likely. Though Vaughan Pendred was far too professional to heap praise where it was not deserved; he would not have compromised his integrity just because Stroudley gave him footplate passes. The *Engineer* said Stroudley's work was good because it had access to the proof.

As the class grew, the 'Terriers' were soon almost monopolising the South London line and as soon as some could be spared they were taking over the East London line too. Again, this line had stations set close together, needing sharp acceleration to manage anything like an acceptable schedule, and it also had the fearsome 1 in 40 gradients on the descent to and climb from the Thames Tunnel. Add in some goods traffic from the sidings serving the docks and industry, as well as a developing through goods traffic between the systems north and south of the Thames, and the picture emerges of a busy line that needed snappy operating. The 'Terriers' soon proved triumphantly that they could cope and would get in nobody's

way. They were also soon found to be just as happy with light goods work as light passenger trains, a good omen for their future.

Even so, and allowing generous time for visits to Brighton Works, maintenance on shed and regular boiler washouts, duties on these two lines alone would not keep busy the 44 'Terriers' based at New Cross and Battersea by 1880. Not even the then prevalent practice of one engine, one crew (which meant, by modern standards, a long working day for the men and a short one for the loco) would account for it. The 'Terriers' were increasingly a feature of other parts of the Brighton's London suburban network. They would work local trains down the main lines as far as Croydon and away from the inner suburban lines they were to be seen on the cluster of routes between Croydon, Wimbledon and Sutton.

Perhaps the most exciting 'Terrier' duty of all was the working of the London Bridge portion of the 'Newhaven Continental', the LBSC's boat train and by any standards a prestige express. The 'Continental' dropped or picked up the London Bridge portion, normally two or three coaches and a mail van, at East Croydon. *Martello* was the regular engine for the down run, quite a challenge for a small engine required to run fast with some severe adverse gradients to climb. The up train was regularly in the charge of *Thames*, which had just 17min to run the $10^{1}/_{4}$ miles start to stop. The modern electric schedules are only a few minutes quicker than that. *Thames* regularly showed her ability to run at 60mph and to be on that engine hurtling down New Cross Bank must have been an exhilarating experience. In terms of revolutions per minute, this was the equivalent of a much more sophisticated Gresley 'A4' Pacific doing over 100mph — quite an achievement for a Victorian tank engine!

It is said that on at least one occasion a 'Terrier' was called on to work a train from London to Brighton, standing for a last-minute failure. It succeeded, thanks to fine enginecraft on the footplate, needing to take water only twice on the way. Stroudley found out (he may even have seen it, as he liked to sit at the bottom of his garden, watching trains pass on the adjacent main line) and is said to have mixed delight and disapproval; at any rate the edict went out that it must not happen again.

Meanwhile, the six non-London members of the class were making their mark too. *Piccadilly*, *Preston* and *Kemptown* were Brighton engines, kept busy on the local services including the Kemp Town branch,[6] *Hailsham* was, appropriately,

at Hailsham, where it worked the local service to Polegate and Eastbourne, while *Bramley* and *Wonersh* were kept at Bramley for the Guildford-Horsham line services, later moving to Horsham Shed. These rural 'Terriers' made an important contribution to 'Terrier' history, for they established that the class was as much at home on rural branch lines as in the suburbs. As 'Terriers' were gradually made redundant in London, there was plenty for them to do elsewhere. In some cases they replaced the last of the Craven relics that had lingered on working branch services and were now long overdue for retirement in favour of something more modern and economical.

One of the disadvantages of being a very small engine is that you can easily be too successful for your own good. The 'Terriers'' great success on the South London line meant that by the early 1880s traffic was increasing to a point beyond their ability. Larger engines, the new 'D' class 0-4-2 tanks, were drafted in to take the heaviest workings but plenty of work remained for the class and the London complement remained unchanged until the mid-1880s. By then trains on the outer suburban lines were getting heavier too and it was becoming evident that on metropolitan work, the 'Terriers' would soon be outliving their usefulness. Initially, plenty could be found for them to do at the LBSC's outer reaches, but how long would it be before they were outclassed there too? When Stroudley had introduced the 'Terriers', they had been given an estimated life of 25 years. In the early 1890s, it looked as if that estimate had been just about right.

⁶It was an oddity of 'Terrier' names that the two-word Kemp Town and Gipsy Hill and Tulse Hill were compressed into single names on engine sides, perhaps reasons of space; with Denmark Hill, the 'Hill' was omitted altogether.

Above:
Shoreditch at New Cross in the 1890s, receiving some attention to dome and Salter valves. The two 'D1' 0-4-2Ts, *Southwark* and *Brockley*, show how much larger were the engines that took over 'Terrier' duties on the London suburban lines.
Lens of Sutton/R. C. Riley Collection

Dimensions as built

Boiler dia	3ft 6in
Boiler length	7ft 10in
Firebox length	4ft 1in
Heating surface:	
Tubes (125 @ 1³⁄₄in)	473 sq ft
Firebox	55 sq ft
Total	528 sq ft
Grate area	10.3 sq ft
Working pressure	140psi
Nom. tractive effort	7,650lb
Cyls	13in x 20in
Coupled wheels	4ft
Wheelbase	6ft + 6ft=12ft
Weight (working order):	
Leading wheels	8ton 4cwt
Centre wheels	8ton 4cwt
Trailing wheels	8ton 4cwt
Total	24ton 12cwt
Water capacity	500gal
Coal capacity	¹⁄₂ton
Overall length	26ft 0¹⁄₂in
Width (running plate)	7ft 2in
Maximum height	11ft 3in

CHAPTER THREE

Later LBSC Years

Steadily increasing train weight was a feature of the latter years of the 19th century and the 'Terriers' were only one of many classes to suffer as a result. They did, in fact, better than most; many fine late Victorian designs, including front line express classes, were outclassed and withdrawn in the 1890s and 1900s as typical train weights soared beyond their capabilities.

Several factors were at work. On the one hand the number of passengers was increasing, as more people had to travel to work rather than live within walking distance, and a steady improvement in working conditions (shorter hours, better pay) meant a gradual growth in leisure travel. Passengers were becoming more discerning and demanding too, helped by competition between companies, which led to improvements in passenger stock. Bogies, corridors, lavatories, more leg-room, more comfortable seats — all these increased the tare weight per passenger carried. Then there were the new legal requirements, such as continuous automatic brakes; up went the weight again.

Not that all these affected short-haul suburban or branch line traffic, of course, especially on the Brighton Railway, which for decades had a reputation for offering the worst rolling stock it thought it could get away with, though every now and then it would turn out something so good that the contrast was glaring.

So in the late 1880s the 'Terriers' were increasingly being redeployed to rural duties and they took to these like ducks to water. Brighton, which could always find plenty for small engines to do, as it met the needs of stations and yards from Lewes to Hove and beyond, added *Hatcham* and *Beulah* to its clutch. Eastbourne, which had had plenty of opportunity to see how useful *Hailsham* could be, got its hands on four, *Leadenhall*, *Tooting*, *Minories* and *Earlswood*, by 1890; though the last would within a few years make its way to Earlswood, where, as the sole resident of an extempore MPD, it worked the bustling yard just south of the Redhill junctions, which then handled a good deal of Brighton/South Eastern exchange traffic.[1]

Below:
Apart from the almost inevitable smokebox stain from the lubricator valve, *Bramley* looks very smart in this 1890s view. Billinton has removed the condenser pipes but it still has wooden brake blocks. The general condition of the loco suggests a recent Works visit.
R. C. Riley Collection

[1]There was no definite policy of placing locomotives at engine sheds of the same name, but if a shed was allocated one with a local name, it would attempt to hang onto it. To suggest that it would be kept cleaner or better maintained than other members of the local stud would be an insult to the high standards of cleanliness and mechanical care that LBSC shed staff worked to as a matter of course.

Above:
Knowle, one of the 'Terriers' sent to Portsmouth in the early 1890s, stands in the depot's coal roads. With clean paint and gleaming brasswork, *Knowle* is almost immaculate apart from paint damage around the boiler clack valve and has acquired iron brake blocks.
Real Photographs/K. Marx Collection

Below:
Knowle is seen at Langstone on the Hayling Island line in 1903. *O. J. Morris/R. C. Riley Collection*

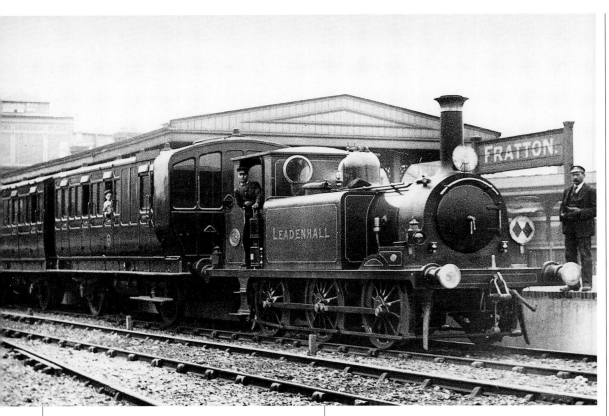

Above left:
Another of the Portsmouth 'Terriers', *Leadenhall* is seen at Fratton with an East Southsea branch train. The 'double diamond' headcode suggests that this is a special working. *Leadenhall* was one of the first 'Terriers' to be scrapped, going shortly after being placed on the duplicate list in mid-1901. *O. J. Morris/ R. C. Riley Collection*

Below;left:
Martello at London Bridge in the 1900s, after being placed on the duplicate list. Its new number is painted on the sidesheet in place of its brass numberplate. The collection of headlamps on the bufferbeam suggest that *Martello* is on pilot duties.
R. C. Riley Collection

Above:
A very workstained *Wapping*, shortly before withdrawal and sale to the KESR. By now back at Brighton shed, the numberplate has again been replaced by a painted duplicate number. *Ian Allan Library*

Below:
Preston was a Brighton engine from the start. It is seen here in Billinton condition at Kemp Town, running round its train. Not surprisingly, this very short branch service was to be an early candidate for motor working. *Ian Allan Library/ Madgwick Collection*

Left:
Kemptown was a 1903 withdrawal and is seen here, stripped of useful fittings, awaiting its fate in the sidings at East Grinstead. Curiously, the brass works plate is still in place on the front splasher. With Brighton chronically short of storage space, withdrawn engines and those well down the queue for Works attention were likely to be banished to underused sidings on quieter parts of the system.
R. C. Riley Collection

Above:
Newly converted to a 2-4-0T for the motor trains experiment, *Boxhill* stands on shed at Brighton. The carrying wheel looks rather incongruous with the splasher and sandbox left in place above it, otherwise the effect is quite harmonious. Carrying Stroudley's goods green livery, other Stroudley features such as name and numberplate have been retained too — all part of the process of making the motor train stock distinctive from the normal fleet. Less satisfactory is the sanding arrangement (new sandboxes ahead of the driving wheels have yet to be fitted) and the experimental nature of the rebuild is underlined by the coupling rod; the fitting for the removed front rod is still in place. Another change is that the buffers have been raised to stand higher above the footplate for better alignment with new stock.
W. G. Tilling/R. C. Riley Collection

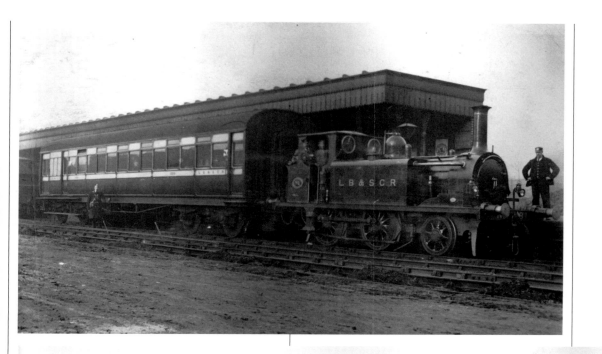

Top:
Beulah by contrast with *Boxhill*, was turned out in the new umber livery for its part in the motor trains experiment. Its feedwater heater was restored and it also kept its Stroudley numberplates. In the light of experience it too soon received repositioned sandboxes, as seen here. It is seen at Kemp Town with one of the new balloon coaches provided for the service. *Ian Allan Library*

Above:
Ranged against the push-pull sets in the trials were a pair of rail-motor units; this is No 1. They proved less than satisfactory in service.
Ian Allan Library/Madgwick Collection

Top:
The other competition, the petrol railcars, were even worse and were soon banished to the Hastings-Eastbourne locals, where they could not do too much harm, before being withdrawn as soon as decently possible.
Ian Allan Library

Above:
A motor service on the Victoria-Sutton route passes Balham Intermediate signalbox. The 'Terrier' is propelling a balloon coach and pulling a six-wheeler. For safety reasons an air-worked whistle has been fitted to the driver's end of the coach.
Ian Allan Library/Bucknall Collection

Above:
Martello heads a Coulsdon-Crystal Palace motor service near Purley in September 1912. The locomotive's size against the balloon coach shows up well and it has now acquired coal rails to increase bunker capacity. *Ken Nunn/Klaus Marx Collection*

Tulsehill and *Merton* went to Midhurst, where they played a large part in working the Chichester-Midhurst-Pulborough line that formed the western boundary of LBSC territory. *Millwall* went to Bognor (the 'Regis' suffix was to come later) and took over from a Craven oddity the working of the Barnham-Bognor branch, *Cheam* went to Epsom, *Knowle* to Tunbridge Wells, *Crowborough* to Newhaven and *Bookham* to Littlehampton. These last two moves were connected with local harbour lines, a rather minor affair at Littlehampton, but Newhaven Harbour was to have a continuous link with the 'Terriers' for nearly 80 years. At this stage the Harbour Company (legally separate from the LBSC but in every way a close working partner) had its own engines but *Crowborough* certainly stood in when needed (and when it could be spared from the Seaford branch, its main duty) and showed in no uncertain way that it was ideal for the work on offer.

Moves away from London and transfers between other sheds continued through the 1890s. Brighton, with a need for station pilots, the Kemp Town branch service and yards to be shunted on the coast lines, managed to keep its fleet at around six to eight. Midhurst increased its allocation to three and the class finally established a presence at the Brighton's western frontier, Portsmouth. Here there was not only plenty of shunting on offer but two branch lines to be worked: East Southsea and one which became synonymous with the 'Terriers', the Hayling Island branch. Portsmouth was in due course replaced by a new, joint LBSC/LSWR shed at Fratton, which was to have a 'Terrier' presence throughout its existence until closure in 1959, specifically because of the Hayling Island line.

Some duties remained in the London area, such as the West Croydon-Wimbledon line and the Kensington and Woodside branches. Battersea and New Cross still held on to 10 or so each through much of the decade. Some were in reserve for their replacements on the suburban services but Battersea had station pilot duties at Victoria to think of, as well as the maze of lines needing pilot and light goods transfer workings in the Battersea/Clapham areas. New Cross covered station pilot duties at London Bridge, as well as

meeting the needs of the East London line and extensive shunting and engineers' train duties in the district. One suspects that few of the London 'Terriers' were idle for long, although by this time other engines, such as the numerous 'D' class 0-4-2Ts, would have been available for many of these duties. Perhaps part of the story is that the engines were retained as long as the sheds could find an excuse, because the men liked them.

But the outclassing of the 'Terriers' as train weights increased was continuing inexorably, in country and coastal sheds as well as the London ones, and in early 1899 an ominous decision was made. The Locomotive Committee agreed to reduce the 'Terrier' fleet to 15 over the next three years. Locomotives would be withdrawn as they came to need heavy work on boilers or fireboxes. As many of the boilers were originals and had served between 20 and 25 years, it was reasonable for the Committee to assume that 30 or more candidates for withdrawal would select themselves over the next few years.

The decision was sensible enough at the time. The amount of work remaining available to 'Terriers' was still in decline and with a growing need for larger engines, the expense of major repairs on small ones could not be justified. A medium-term future for 'Terriers' could only be seen on a few branch line services and as shed and works pilots.

What is now harder to understand is why the Locomotive Committee overlooked what was soon to become obvious — that redundant 'Terriers' were marketable commodities. *Fenchurch*, the first to enter traffic, had become the first to be sold, to the Newhaven Harbour Co in mid-1898, having just achieved its 25-year accountancy life-expectancy. That sale can be viewed as more of a paper transfer involving money to keep the auditors happy (the companies were hand in glove and remained separate only because a legal requirement forbade a merger or takeover), so the Committee could be excused for not taking the point that other railways might be glad to buy 'Terriers'. However, when the Isle of Wight Central Railway had to ask — almost beg — to be allowed to buy a used 'Terrier' before the LBSC would take its request seriously, one would have thought that the message might have got through — particularly when the Central came back and bought three more! This seemed to do it and 'Terriers' were advertised for sale, with some success.

Withdrawals for scrapping were proceeding, however. Eleven went between 1901 and 1904, sold to a scrap merchant for £125 each. By contrast with the £500 to £800 that 'Terriers' were fetching on the second-hand market, it might seem that scrapping was a poor bargain. However, as the new owners were paying for working locomotives, which often had quite substantial attention at Brighton Works before dispatch to their new homes, compared with the largely worn-out machines that were dismantled at Redhill and elsewhere, the Brighton was probably not striking such a bad bargain after all.

With 11 scrapped and 15 sold to new owners, quite a dent had been made in the 'Terrier' fleet but it seems that it was not declining fast enough for the Locomotive Committee, who decided to get nasty and identified 15 'Terriers' for withdrawal in 1905/6, as well as signing the warrants for a few that had been withdrawn and stored. So by 1906 the Brighton's stock of 'Terriers' might well have been reduced to single figures, with a fair chance of extinction on its home territory within a few more years, but for a remarkable and, for the 'Terriers', lucky change of fortune.

In a nutshell, the Brighton was in a bad box. For some years the net income had been falling, as costs rose without revenue rising in proportion. New threats to revenue were now emerging in the form of competition. To survive, the company would have to take strong action.

The rising costs were largely beyond its control. As mentioned, train weight per passenger had risen enormously in the past 30 years, which meant bigger engines, higher fuel bills, perhaps even more trains to run. New labour laws had reduced the hours that staff could be required to work and the trades unions were starting to find their powers and resisting commensurate wage cuts, or even pressing for pay rises. This affected not just the railway but its suppliers; the cost of coal, for instance, was rising, as pay and conditions in the mines improved. And of course, just to maintain services at the same level, an increase in staff numbers was unavoidable.

The company could of course have passed this on to customers in the form of higher fares and goods rates. But the conviction among a large proportion of the public that transport companies

Below:
Not all push-pull services were on busy main lines. *Beulah*, still in 2-4-0T form, is seen on a Sheffield Park-Lewes service at Newick & Chailey.
A. H. Homewood/Madgwick Collection

are in control of a gigantic rip-off and profiteering like mad, was as prevalent then as now. Public opposition to price rises was likely to be strong. And meanwhile the shareholders were getting restless.

As if that were not enough, the Brighton's monopoly on its own patch was being challenged. A scheme to build a rival London-Brighton express line had made considerable progress. Proposing a high-speed electric line, it promised a significantly faster service than the Brighton was offering. The company hit back with a stage-managed and highly publicised high speed run from London to Brighton which, at just over 48min, undercut the times the new scheme was proposing. It scared the rivals off. True, the Brighton did not change its schedules but it had made the point that it could if it wanted to, and the scheme died; it was too risky an investment.

Other competition, however, was much harder to deal with. Mechanised road transport was just starting to appear and the particularly deadly competitor in large urban areas was the electric tram. Its greater convenience and lower fares than a railway could offer attracted workers and shoppers away from the trains and in South London especially it was soon making a serious inroad on passenger revenue. Trams had already arrived in Brighton and the potential for a tramway system linking the spread of towns along the coast to Worthing was not lost on the Brighton directors. In London they had to react; perhaps on the coast they could get their blow in first. A way of operating frequent, low-cost trains was needed.

The solution in the London suburbs was overhead electrification, which eventually spread down from the main termini as far as Coulsdon and Sutton. But on the coast, and on branch lines where profits were getting dangerously low, the high initial capital cost of electrification could not be justified. The answer lay in cheaper steam, or perhaps internal combustion, operation.

So the Brighton went down the path being trodden by a number of companies but perhaps more scientifically than most. Push-pull operation of one- or two-coach trains should allow considerable savings. Small, economical engines with nippy acceleration would be needed. Suddenly the 'Terriers' had a new role. However, to be certain, the company adapted just two of the class for their new duties, buying for comparison two steam railcars and two petrol railcars. These proved more expensive to operate than a 'Terrier' on a push-pull coach — and far more prone to breakdowns. The threat of obliteration of the 'Terriers' was withdrawn.

Douglas Earle Marsh was now in charge at Brighton and he quickly got down to sorting out

Below:
Showing what a 'Terrier' can do on a fairly level road, *Whitechapel* runs into Barnham with a train from Bognor in 1914.
O. J. Morris/Ian Allan Library

Above:
At the very end of Marsh's tenure at Brighton, the new 'Terrier' boiler and smokebox was designed which converted the engines to 'A1X' class. *Wonersh* was one of the first two rebuilt, in November 1911. It is seen in full Marsh livery with gilt numerals on the bunker side but still retaining its Stroudley chimney. *R. C. Riley Collection*

the 'Terriers' for their new role. The trouble he took shows that he did not view this as a distraction from more important developments elsewhere; but it is interesting to note that experience showed him that he could not improve much on Stroudley's original concept.

Boxhill and *Beulah* were the pair selected for the trial conversions. They were still much as built, except that Billinton had removed the feedwater heating system, which he felt gave more trouble than advantage. The pair were converted to 2-4-0Ts by removing the front wheelset and replacing it with a pair of smaller, plain wheels, modifying the axlebox arrangements to suit. Quite what this was meant to achieve is still a subject for debate but it was clearly experimental, for the original splashers were left in place, looking rather out of proportion. So were the sandboxes, which soon proved to be a mistake, for the sand was largely lost by the time the first driven wheel reached it, and so new sandboxes were fitted, mounted under the footplate and just ahead of the driving wheels. Also, while the front section of coupling rod was removed, the rear section retained the pivot hole at which it was attached, in case the process was reversed. On *Boxhill* the cylinders were sleeved down from 13in to nine, which was close to the size of those on the steam railcars; the whole operation seems to have been intended to reduce the power of the locomotive to suit its one-coach duties, for which removing the front coupled wheels would make sense as it would reduce the mechanical resistance slightly while still giving enough bite at the four remaining driven wheels to give adequate adhesion for a one-coach train. Mechanical driving links from the remote end of the trailer car were installed, and a shriller whistle was fitted in the hopes that its sound would carry better past the bulk of the coach when propelling.[2]

Boxhill, the first of the pair to re-enter traffic, also had its boiler pressure reduced to 130psi. This was clearly found to be overdoing things a little, for when *Beulah* commenced trials two months later, it kept its 150psi boiler pressure and had its cylinders sleeved down just to 12in. It also had its feedwater heaters restored; Marsh was out for every economy he could get.

Another curious feature was the livery. *Beulah* was painted in the newly approved Marsh livery of lined umber, with its name replaced by the initials LB&SCR. *Boxhill* by contrast carried Stroudley goods green and kept its name. It is tempting to suggest that this was a way of using up old paint stocks but there was more to it than

---

[2]*It was only partially successful. The push-pull trains developed a reputation for creeping up on people, catching lineside workers and trespassers unawares, occasionally with serious consequences.*

Above:
The appearance of the first of Lawson Billinton's express Baltic Tanks (big machines for their day) in 1914 gave the LBSC the opportunity to indulge in some 'little and large' photographs. Here the prototype Baltic, *Charles C. Macrae*, is posed with *Boxhill* at Lovers Walk, Brighton. *Klaus Marx Collection*

that. Several railways which introduced either railcar or push-pull services painted them in a livery distinct from the standard passenger colours, to reinforce the message to the public that here was something new and worth their attention. The Brighton was sounding out public opinion as well as testing the economics of this new concept and the use of an unusual livery for a passenger engine was in part at least a test of public reaction.

It was one test that did not stand proven and Marsh umber became standard for motor-fitted 'Terriers' along with the rest of the passenger fleet. Likewise, the 2-4-0T conversion was not found to give any real benefit — in fact it limited the ability of the engine to be sent off on other duties if required — and was not repeated. *Beulah* and *Boxhill* were converted back to 0-6-0Ts in 1913. The 12in cylinders and restoration of feedwater heating were successful economy measures and were repeated in the other 'Terriers' that were fitted with motor controls.

Between 1906 and 1909 another 20 'Terriers' were adapted for push-pull working, effectively lifting the threat of individual withdrawal and class extinction. Further proof that the class was once again seen to have a future was the decision in 1911 to build new boilers. This was in effect a rebuild, the only one the class ever underwent. Much the same in dimensions as the original, and

at least as good a steam generator, the new boiler was accompanied by a new and larger smokebox, this time cylindrical and sitting on a cast saddle. Accompanying this change, the high front sandboxes were removed, and replaced with a plain segmental front splasher, new sandboxes being fitted below the running plate. On the boiler, the dome was a few inches further forward than before but retained the Salter safety valves.

Marsh's reboilerings of other Stroudley classes featured the fitting of a fatter dome and safety valves over the firebox, but left the smokeboxes, with their wing-plates and sand boxes, unaltered. We can now only speculate on whether Marsh felt that a longer smokebox would be a really worthwhile improvement on the 'Terriers', or whether he, like others, was developing a bit of a soft spot for these little engines and thought that they deserved a little more time and trouble in the drawing office.

Under Stroudley the 'Terriers' had been listed as Class A. To Marsh's ordered, Doncaster-trained mind this was not precise enough and they became 'A1'. The rebuilt, reboilered engines were reclassified as 'A1X', the official term by which they have been known ever since. A number of owners of the 'sold Terriers' also acquired new boilers from the LBSC for their engines, which led to a slightly confusing situation as not all were given the full 'A1X' treatment. Various intermediate stages can be found to this day.

As the 'Terriers' were converted, the motor train service was expanded. The Brighton's philosophy was not so much to replace existing services as to use the 'motors' to increase service frequency. This was done in urban areas to compete with the frequent and cheap road transport and on rural lines to meet the demands for more trains at a low cost. The service on some country branches was so sparse that it is not surprising that there were complaints. Just five or six return trips per day was not unknown, which was hardly enough to stimulate the local economy. The 'motors' could add three or four trips to this and while it was not going to bring hordes onto the trains (they did not exist) it at least helped to increase goodwill.

As well as the Worthing-Brighton service, the Kemp Town branch was soon turned over to motor working (almost exclusively in this case) and a Lewes-Seaford service was introduced. The Hayling Island line was handed over to push-pull and a Chichester-Portsmouth link improved the service offered at that end of the West Coast line. Services were introduced from Tunbridge Wells to Oxted, East Grinstead and Uckfield and from Horsham to Horley via Three Bridges. The Eastbourne area saw them taking over the Hailsham locals and working Eastbourne-St Leonards services on the East Coast line. Among other special services was a Lewes-Sheffield Park run mornings and afternoons partly for the benefit of school children.

Even the London area saw motor trains, with West Croydon to Belmont and to Wimbledon and the Tooting-Wimbledon lines being largely motor-worked in the years leading up to World War 1.

Extra halts were opened on the motor train routes, specifically for these trains; their good power-to-weight ratio allowed the 'Terriers' to retain their reputation for snappy acceleration, so these extra stops could be made without delaying the main passenger services on the route.

To work with the 'Terriers' on these services, Marsh turned out some of the largest coaches ever built by the LBSC. The company had for years ignored the move towards higher and wider coach bodies that most other lines were making and its standard stock still had a profile more typical of the 1880s. Panter, who was Marsh's Carriage & Wagon Superintendent, was to change things so far as he was allowed. New coaches that took better advantage of the loading gauge were turned out for the Brighton's two extremes of traffic: the most prestigious fast trains such as the 'City Limited' and the push-pulls. Passengers elsewhere continued to put up with rather more cramped quarters.

Easy to identify by their bulbous elliptical roofs rather than the Brighton's normal arc profile, the new push-pull coaches were promptly nicknamed 'Balloons'. Their insides were not quite so luxurious as the outside suggested, somewhat unyielding upholstery and a rather cosy closeness of passengers when fully loaded being typical features. Their other characteristic, it must be said, was the rather comical sight that these large coaches presented when coupled to the smallest passenger engines on the system; it was rather reminiscent of a tug coping with a large liner, or a small dog pushing an elephant round the place.

Relative aesthetics apart, the LBSC had come up with a winning combination. The economies achieved were not quite as good as had been hoped, partly because plans to reduce staffing levels came to nothing[3], but traffic was held on to and indeed increased on most motor-served routes. So far as the 'Terriers' were concerned, they had found and mastered a new niche in the nick of time. True, once again in some cases the new services became so popular that more coaches and larger engines had to be drafted in to cope, but there was no more talk of mass withdrawals.

When Lawson Billinton (son of Robert) took over from Marsh, he left the 'Terriers' well alone, continuing to have Marsh boilers built as required. The livery was slightly simplified, with the tankside lettering reduced to just 'LBSC', but otherwise little changed, either in terms of appearance or duties. For the rest of the Brighton's existence as an independent company, the class's future was more secure than it had been at the turn of the century.

[3]The Board of Trade flatly refused a proposal that the roles of fireman and guard be carried out by one person.

Dimensions as rebuilt (Class A1X)

Boiler dia		3ft 6in
Boiler length		8ft 1in
Firebox length		4ft 1in
Heating surface:		
	Tubes (119 @ 1³/₄in)	433 sq ft
	Firebox	55¹/₂sq ft
	Total	488¹/₂sq ft
Grate area		10 sq ft
Working pressure		150psi
Weight:		
	Empty	23ton 10cwt
	Working order	26ton 15cwt
Fully loaded:		
	Leading wheels	8ton 0cwt
	Centre wheels	10ton 5cwt
	Trailing wheels	10ton 0cwt
	Total	28ton 5cwt

(cyl bore varied between class members)

Above left:
Tulsehill was one of the 'Terriers' transferred to departmental service in Brighton days, in its case from 1919. It is seen in plain black departmental livery, shorn of its number and even its works plate, in Battersea Loco yard.
Ian Allan Library/Madgwick Collection

Left:
Still an 'A1' but with other changes apparent, *Morden* is seen inside the roundhouse at Fratton in May 1920. Fratton was to be home to the largest number of 'Terriers' right up to its closure in 1959.
H. C. Casserley

Withdrawals (LBSCR)

NO.	NAME	WITHDRAWN	FATE
72	Fenchurch	1898	Sold, Newhaven Hbr Co
75	Blackwall	1899	Sold, IWCR
69	Peckham	1900	Sold, IWCR
648	Leadenhall	1901	Scrapped
51	Rotherhithe	1901	Scrapped
65	Tooting	1901	Scrapped
66	Hatcham	1901	Scrapped
70	Poplar	1901	Sold, KESR
36	Bramley	1902	Sold, Pauling & Co
39	Denmark	1902	Sold, Pauling & Co
40	Brighton	1902	Sold, IWCR
41	Piccadilly	1902	Scrapped
649	Bishopsgate	1902	Sold, Pauling & Co
652	Surrey	1902	Sold, Pauling & Co
657	Thames	1902	Sold, Pauling & Co
658	Wandle	1902	Scrapped
660	Ewell	1902	Scrapped
664	Kemptown	1902	Scrapped
646	Newington	1903	Sold, LSWR
656	Shoreditch	1903	Scrapped
68	Clapham	1903	Sold, LSWR
76	Hailsham	1903	Scrapped
84	Crowborough	1903	Sold, IWCR
645	Merton	1904	Scrapped
654	Waddon	1904	Sold, SECR
671	Wapping	1905	Sold, KESR
638	Millwall	1906	Trs service dept stock; sold to WD 1918
637	Southdown	1908	Trs service dept stock; sold to WD 1918
679	Minories	1918	Sold, WD
681	Beulah	1918	Sold, WD
683	Earlswood	1918	Sold, WD
642	Tulsehill	1919	Trs service dept
673	Deptford	1919	Sold, EHLR
682	Boxhill	1919	Trs service dept
667	Brixton	1920	Sold, industrial service
674	Shadwell	1920	Sold, EHLR

NB — Duplicate List (600 series) numbers given where applied. List is in original LBSC numerical order for each year

CHAPTER FOUR

Off the Beaten Track — the Years in the Backwaters

Over a third of the whole 'Terrier' class was to be sold to new operators in the Brighton's last 25 years. This probably constitutes a record for any sizeable class on a British railway, pre- or post-Grouping.

The new owners were a mixed bunch, though a sizeable number of the sales were to lines connected with the memorable Col H. Stephens. What they had in common was the need for small but competent engines, in good order, at a budget price. In the 'Terriers' they made good bargains. And it was not the fault of the locomotives that some of them went expensively wrong after purchase. After all, their sisters still on home metals kept running, despite often having higher annual mileages.

An untypical sale, which led to an unexpected career, was the first of all. *Fenchurch*, the first of the class to enter service, was sold to the Newhaven Harbour Co in mid-1898, having just passed its 25th anniversary of service.

Newhaven was the Brighton's cross-channel port, operated in direct (and reasonably successful) competition with Dover and Folkestone, and also a busy freight port. The Newhaven Harbour Co was independent from the railway company only because the legal position

demanded it and in fact the two were so closely entwined that you had to look hard to see the join! With a network of lines and sidings on both sides of the harbour, linked by a tramway over the swingbridge that adjoined Newhaven Town station, the Harbour Co needed steam power and owned a couple of small saddle tanks. By the mid-1890s these were evidently getting increasingly troublesome and costly to maintain, for their visits to Brighton Works were getting more frequent and expensive. One of the pair finally gave up the ghost in 1898 and the company, which had borrowed the resident Newhaven 'Terrier' on occasions before, hired *Peckham* while making arrangements for something more permanent. The Brighton soon agreed to sell *Fenchurch*, which was put through Brighton Works before despatch to Newhaven that June, for the princely sum of £350.

Fenchurch lost its numberplate and Westinghouse brake but was otherwise little changed, retaining Stroudley livery and the name. Links with its birthplace were not really severed either, for when major work was needed it was always packed off back to Brighton. Indeed, one gets the impression that the financial side of the sale was more to satisfy the accountants, tax

inspectors and other late Victorian prodnoses, who might otherwise have asked awkward questions and drawn the wrong (or perhaps the right?) conclusions.

Fenchurch was to spend the next 57 years at Newhaven, broken only by trips to Brighton Works and a few excursions elsewhere in later years. In that time it became a local institution, with its regular crossings of the swingbridge, preceded by a man on foot ringing a handbell (after World War 2 this practice was abandoned in favour of closing the bridge to all other traffic when a train was crossing). Mileage as sold was just under 600,000 and though it increased more slowly thereafter, the wear and tear of start-stop shunting work took its toll. In 1904 it was fitted with new, 14-inch cylinders and apparently was returned still carrying Stroudley yellow livery and name. By the time of its next visit, 1910, stocks of yellow and green paint were long exhausted and *Fenchurch* went home painted black, picked out with double red border lines. Surprisingly, it still

kept its name, painted in pale yellow in its accustomed place. Rebuilding to 'A1X' followed in 1913 and in 1917 the little black engine finally lost its name, though it was replaced with the legend 'Newhaven Harbour Company' a few years later. It made little difference; *Fenchurch* it was and *Fenchurch* it remained to the railway and harbour staff, and the people of Newhaven.

The recently-formed Southern Railway finally gained the powers to absorb the Newhaven Harbour Co in 1926 and duly did so, bringing *Fenchurch* back into the fold at the same time. Given a book value of £575 (which says more about the onset of 20th century inflation than a jump in its value since 1898), the engine visited Brighton Works that December, emerging in SR black goods livery and carrying a number again for the first time in 28 years. Herein was an oddity though; *Fenchurch* would logically have become No B672, taking its old place in the class list; instead it was allotted B636 (taking *Bramley's* place, that 'Terrier' having been withdrawn, sold

Left:
IWC No 10 (*Peckham*) stands by the Newport coal heap; it is in the later IWC lined black livery, with the company name in full in shaded letters. Still largely in original condition, complete with wooden brake blocks.
R. C. Riley Collection

Left:
IWC No 10 arrives at Ventnor Town (later West) with a set of ex-LSWR coaches. *Isle of Wight Steam Railway Collection*

Below:
Crowborough as IWC No 12 in the final livery with simplified lettering. It has been rebuilt to 'A1X' with the splasher sandboxes retained (a sign of a non-Brighton Works rebuild) and the bunker has been extended to the rear bufferbeam — which became a standard alteration for 'Island Terriers'. The locally-cast chimney blends quite well with the rest of the engine.
LPC/Ian Allan Library

Left:
'Terriers' in industrial service were rarely photographed but *Bishopsgate* was recorded while working on Pauling's Northolt contract. It retains Stroudley livery, with Pauling's identity above the name. The smokebox locking dart has been at least augmented by a strap and bolt, visible beside the lubricator pot. Curiously, the locomotive behind, Manning Wardle 0-6-0ST *Northolt*, was to have a long association with 'Terriers', as it was sold to the Freshwater, Yarmouth & Newport in 1913 and served on the Isle of Wight for nearly 20 years. *Bishopsgate* had no such luck, being scrapped in 1909.
R. C. Riley Collection

Left:
Wapping, the second 'Terrier' sold to the Kent & East Sussex, is seen early in its career on that line, with its new name *Rolvenden* and company name painted on the tankside. Seen at Rolvenden yard, it is in early KESR blue livery; vacuum brake has replaced air but otherwise it is in Billinton condition, including wooden brake blocks.
F. Moore/R. C. Riley Collection

and later scrapped), subsequently becoming No 2636 and finally BR No 32636.

Fenchurch continued to rule the roost on the Newhaven sidings, joined through the later 1930s and 1940s by *Cheapside*, which gives an idea of how much traffic the port was handling at the time. In 1950 it received yet another new livery, this time BR lined black, which was supposed to denote secondary passenger service. True, this was the normal livery of the capital stock 'Terriers' and corresponded with their work elsewhere, but it seemed a bit like a case of rigid interpretation of rules when applied to a locomotive that had been confined to Newhaven docks for over half a century and had last worked a passenger train in the 1890s!

That was to change, however, with the engine's minor 'celebrity' status. Now definitely an institution at Newhaven, and introduced to Richard Dimbleby for a BBC radio programme, this little engine was attracting wider attention and was even getting requests to haul special trains. Someone in BR decided that it was high time *Fenchurch* earned its livery, and it was duly despatched to Eastbourne in July 1952 for a week on local passenger services. This was a prelude to a series of specials in the Brighton area as well as its usual duties at Newhaven.

The situation changed in October 1955 when *Fenchurch* finally left the town that had been its home for nearly 60 years, and moved to St Leonards for duties on the Kent & East Sussex. This line had been the haunt of 'Terriers' for years but was now reduced to goods-only, with occasional special passenger workings. *Fenchurch* was to potter about on these services for several years, before leaving to join its class sisters at Fratton in late 1959, and see out its BR days on the last 'Terrier' duty of all, the Hayling Island branch.

Left:
Bodiam needed further attention later that year and was despatched to Brighton Works. It is seen before return, gleaming in fresh green paint, in quite exalted company. At last a vacuum ejector exhaust pipe to the smokebox has been fitted, replacing the previous arrangement of a short pipe running up the cab front to exhaust at roof level.
Real Photographs/ Klaus Marx Collection

Below left:
Newly sold to the LSWR, *Newington* is now simply No 734 but otherwise has had little beyond a change in livery and conversion to vacuum brake before entering service. *H. Gordon Tidey/ Bucknall Collection*

Below:
Hired (and later sold) to the Freshwater, Yarmouth & Newport, *Newington* is seen on the barge that transported it across the Solent, along with several of the coaches that the FYN had to buy from the Great Central in an equal hurry, in its frantic efforts to maintain its services following its row with the IoW Central.
R. C. Riley Collection

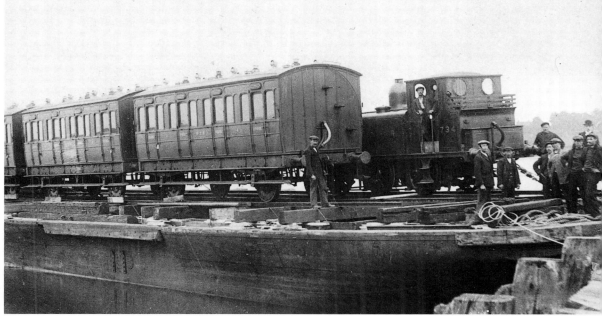

If *Fenchurch* had an unexpectedly long second career, the next few 'Terriers' to be sold were to establish an important 'second home' for the class. Service on the Isle of Wight was an important factor in keeping up class numbers through to the 1940s.

The Isle of Wight had developed a surprisingly large railway network for a small, mainly rural and lightly-populated island. One result of this was that traffic, outside the then short holiday season[1], was light and profits were low. Of the three railway companies on the island, the Isle of Wight Railway, with its main line from Ryde to Ventnor and a single short branch, was reasonably prosperous; the Isle of Wight Central, which operated a Cowes-Newport-Ryde main line, a Newport-Sandown secondary route and a remote branch to the unfashionable end of Ventnor, was just able to keep its head above water; and the Freshwater, Yarmouth & Newport Railway lived on a financial knife-edge.

By the end of the 19th century the IWC, which had been managing with an ageing motive power fleet including some fairly dubious second-hand purchases, urgently needed to buy more, to allow the worst of its relics to be retired and take the strain off the rest of the fleet. The problem was

the almost complete lack of ready money. Obviously, any purchase would have to be second-hand again. So the IWC set about the depressing business of writing to main line companies, asking if they had any surplus, used but serviceable engines going cheap. The replies were not encouraging; it is recorded that that from Brighton fell little short of being rude. But the IWC was clearly aware that some 'Terriers' were being earmarked as surplus and knew the reputation of the class, so it tried again. Persistence brought its reward and in March 1899 the LBSC sold *Blackwall* to the IWC for £800; a notably higher price than *Fenchurch's* transfer fee and reflecting not only a more realistic valuation but also the very thorough overhaul it received at Brighton before dispatch to the island. Even so, the IWC, which had been prepared to spend more if it absolutely had to and had haggled hard about the price, had to buy the engine through an

Below:
Clapham remained in the LSWR fleet, mainly for use in the Portsmouth area. It is seen here at Eastleigh, after acquiring a Drummond boiler in 1912. On the cab roof are the pulleys and wires for the LSWR push-pull control, the wires running forward via a support mounted on the safety valve to a pair of loops on the chimney; the whole system seemed to owe more to Heath Robinson than to normal railway engineering standards! *R. C. Riley Collection*

[1]*Until the late 1930s the British holiday season lasted for less than two months, from mid-July to early September.*

intermediary, the Southern Counties Rolling Stock Finance Co; the steam engine equivalent of buying a car on hire-purchase. In fact, this company was set up by a few IWC directors, specifically to finance the purchase of stock for the line without too much risk to themselves (which suggests a certain lack of confidence in the viability of their own company!) and it played its part in all the IWC's 'Terrier' purchases.

Blackwall delighted its new owners. Too small for further LBSC duties it might have been, but it was larger and more powerful than most of its IWC stablemates and, even more exciting, it was in good mechanical order. (Sadly, it was kept so busy that this latter did not last and Newport could not afford to maintain its locomotives to the same standard as Brighton Works.) It soon proved that it could work all IWC trains bar the heaviest summer loads on the Cowes-Ryde run, and was economical to operate on the already unprofitable

Ventnor branch. Like Oliver Twist, the IWC was soon asking the Brighton for more; possibly it expected a similar response but Billinton, with surplus 'Terriers' on his hands and plenty of spares in the Works, was mellowing. Over the next few years the IWC was able to buy three more 'Terriers': *Peckham* for £700 in 1900, *Brighton* for £600 in 1902 and *Crowborough* for £725 in 1903. All passed through Brighton Works on their way to Newport and the sale price reflected the amount of work carried out. At last the IWC had a class of broadly identical engines which were capable of working nearly any duty on the line.

They became Nos 9-12 on the IWC, losing their names but looking very smart in the rich red livery, with the tanks adorned by the company name in a garter encircling the number. In due course the red was replaced by black, with the name in full across the tank sides, later replaced by large initials.

Left:
Dido (*Millwall*) had by contrast been put out to grass when photographed amid other relics of long-gone S&M stock. The bunker extension is interesting, as are the sheet metal shields fitted to protect the rear spectacle glasses.
M. D. England/
R. C. Riley Collection

Left:
S&M *Daphne* was sold to the SR in 1939 and went to Eastleigh to provide spares for other 'Terriers'. The slow cannibalisation was well under way when it was photographed in company with the last of the Beattie 0-6-0STs, in the Works scrap siding in May 1946.
R. C. Riley Collection

Right:
'A1X' *Deptford* (and *Shadwell's* bunker) at the Stratford shed of the S&MJR. The pair went to Stratford at weekends for maintenance and it is rumoured that the S&M occasionally sneaked a few service trips out of them! *R. C. Riley Collection*

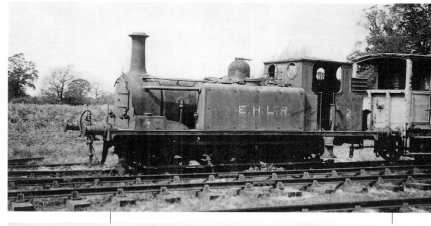

Right:
Still an 'A1', *Shadwell* stands abandoned by all except a caretaker after the EHLR's closure. Traces of its former LBSC identity are showing through the EHLR livery.
R. C. Riley Collection

Right:
The other 'Terrier' to go to industrial service was *Brixton*, which went to Grassmore Colliery, Chesterfield, and was named *Ashgate*. It suffered various alterations to fit it for its new duties; it is seen here in the colliery yard, a bit grubby but otherwise apparently in good order.
J. M. Jarvis/
R. C. Riley Collection

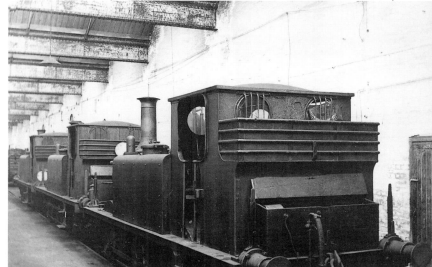

Right:
The Southern Railway had a surplus of 'Terriers' on its formation in 1923. Three are seen withdrawn and stored in Brighton Works paintshop, pending a decision about the future. Nearest the camera are *Knowle* and *Stepney*, both of which were reprieved and returned to service.
M. D. England/
R. C. Riley Collection

Things became brighter after the Grouping, when the 'Terriers' were given full SR lined green livery. Another good marketing touch was that the island's locomotive fleet were named, all names being of island towns or villages. Of these four 'Terriers', *Blackwall* became *Carisbrooke*, *Peckham* became *Cowes*, *Brighton* became *Newport* and *Crowborough* became *Ventnor*. One curiosity was that they kept the IWC numbers for the rest of their island careers; the SR, and BR after it, left the Isle of Wight system with its own numbering series, never integrating it with mainland stock. Starting at No W1, it reached W36, engines being given island numbers when they arrived, and reverting to their original numbers if they returned to the mainland for further service.

In due course the IWC foursome were rebuilt to 'A1Xs', new boilers coming from Brighton when the old ones wore out. One significant change, which marked them apart from their mainland sisters, was the enlarging of the bunkers. This process began in late IWC days and was also carried out on subsequent arrivals under SR auspices. By removing the rear tool box and extending the bunker back to the buffer beam, the coal capacity was doubled and the number of trips back to the shed for refuelling were reduced accordingly, saving time and mileage. It was a most useful modification and was left in place on island 'Terriers' that returned to mainland service, though it was not felt sufficiently valuable to convert, say, the rest of the Fratton fleet to match. *Martello*, never an island engine, did eventually acquire an

Above:
Ashtead, seen at Littlehampton in February 1927, makes a good study of an 'A1X' in early SR condition. The 'B' (for Brighton) number was the first form of SR fleet numbering, until a full renumbering took place in the early 1930s. *H. C. Casserley*

Below:
Boxhill entered the SR era already ensconced as the Brighton Works pilot. Still in lined umber, it has acquired a 'Southern Railway B' motif on the bunker. Less official are at least three buckets and several oil cans on the tank top, odd bits of timber packing on the front footplate, a large hook on the smokebox handrail and a bag of something tied to the cab handrail. *LPC/Ian Allan Library*

island bunker, by the chance of going through Eastleigh Works after one had been dismantled outside, but this was a unique occurrence.

Another sign of an 'Island A1X' was that it retained its original front sandboxes, sitting alongside the new smokebox saddle. Whether this was better than the Brighton rearrangement or not is a matter of locomotive aesthetics, discussion of which is one of the things that keeps the British brewing industry profitable!

Returning to the Brighton and the early 1900s, other sales were made, Billinton's advertising having borne fruit. The civil engineering contractors Pauling & Co bought five — *Bramley, Denmark, Bishopsgate, Surrey* and *Thames* — for £670 each. They were put to work on Pauling's major job of the time, construction of the Great Central's Northolt-High Wycombe section. All were apparently in fairly good order and represented a good deal to Pauling, who would otherwise have either been buying new industrial tank engines for considerably more, or second-hand industrial machines, redundant at the end of a contract and probably in very dubious condition. The five were adapted for life on a far more basic railway than they were accustomed to; dumb buffers (square blocks of hardwood) were fitted to match the primitive contractor's wagons in use at the time, the guard irons were removed, as more a hindrance than a help on erratic temporary track, and tyre washers were fitted, to reduce the likelihood of derailments caused by the build-up of debris where the track was awash with mud.

They managed several years' hard work before disposal. *Bramley, Denmark* and *Bishopsgate* went for scrap in 1909, worn out even by contractors' loco standards. *Surrey* and *Thames* were sold for further work and according to Bradley went to South America and an unrecorded fate. Poor *Thames*; what a comedown from those early years and the regular flight down New Cross Bank with the 'Newhaven Continental'!

Two other sales were of far more significance for the long-term future of the class. In 1901 *Poplar* was sold to the infant Kent & East Sussex Railway[2], which was so pleased with its purchase that it bought another, *Wapping*, in 1905. Who

Below:
By 1928 *Boxhill* had been tidied up with a change to plain black, loss of the condensing pipes, fitting of dual braking, a Marsh chimney and, curiously, steam heating. *Real Photographs/Ian Allan Library*

[2]At that stage still named the Rother Valley Railway.

could have imagined, at the opening of the 20th century, that *Poplar*, as *Bodiam*, would be still active on the same railway nearly 100 years later?

The Kent & East Sussex was an early venture of that extraordinary luminary of British minor railways, Colonel H. F. Stephens[3]. Like most of his lines, it was a marginal affair, providing a railway where one could barely be justified by the traffic potential. It was built as lightly and cheaply as was legally possible and once operating its knife-edge finances made the IWC look positively prosperous. Stephens, who turned the purchase of used locomotives for his various lines into an art form, made some good choices, some acceptable ones and a number of dramatically unsuitable ones. The 'Terriers' were among his best bargains, being almost ideal for the level and make-up of traffic on offer and robust enough to take the indifferent maintenance that poverty was to force on them.

To be an engineer on a Stephens line one needed wide workshop skills, considerable ability in make-do-and-mend, practical knowledge of applying the verb 'to cannibalise' and the patience to put up with a boss who (to judge by some surviving records) modelled his labour relations style on that of I. K. Brunel on a bad day. But even these paragons (and minor railway engineers were often more accomplished, in their way, than their counterparts in a big company's main works) found some tasks beyond them and then the assistance of Big Brother, who still owned and maintained 'Terriers', was invoked, to

[3]*He is commonly known as Col Stephens, although he did not receive his commission until World War 1, when he served in the Territorial Army.*

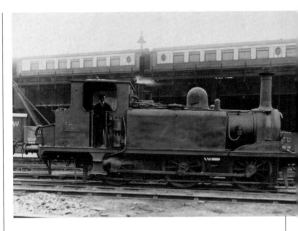

Above:
Waddon returned to familiar haunts post-Grouping and is seen at Battersea Yard, carrying the plain grey livery of its final SECR years. *Ian Allan Library*

Below:
The Newhaven harbour lines remained a 'Terrier' stronghold and long-term resident *Fenchurch* is seen running off railway property and onto the tramway leading to the swing bridge and the West Quay lines in September 1947. Its number is in ex-LBSC gilt numerals; in 1935 a small cache of these was discovered and *Fenchurch* was one of the engines to which they were applied, keeping them until repainted in 1950. *C. C. B. Herbert/R. C. Riley Collection*

Below right:
Cheapside joined *Fenchurch* at Newhaven in 1936 and remained there until shortly before its withdrawal in 1951. It is seen on the tidemills sidings in the later Maunsell livery which it carried until the end, and with the Drummond chimney which a number of 'Terriers' acquired and which always looked a bit too bulky on them. *C. C. B. Herbert/R. C. Riley Collection*

keep the Stephens 'Terriers' in service for longer than was usual with Stephens's stable of assorted cast-offs.

The KESR ran from Robertsbridge, on the South Eastern's Tonbridge-Hastings line, for about 10 relatively level miles along the Rother Valley, then featured a long climb at 1 in 50 to reach Tenterden. From there a more undulating section extended to Headcorn (on the South Eastern again, this time on the Tonbridge-Ashford line). After initial promise, traffic settled down to a level that trains of one coach and a few goods wagons could manage. Passengers fumed while the train engine broke its journey to shunt the goods yards at the stations; those who could afford to bought cars instead and the rest were relieved when the Colonel introduced light petrol railcars for the passenger services — they might have been uncomfortable but at least they got on with the journey.

Poplar and *Wapping*, renamed *Bodiam* and *Rolvenden*, got quietly on with the job of keeping this valuable but under-used and under-resourced byway operating for a quarter of a century and more, until by the early 1930s they were

Above:
Three 'Terriers' line up at Fratton in May 1933. From the left: *Stepney* (still with the LSWR-style push-pull clutter on its cab), *Fulham* and *Morden*.

thoroughly worn out and only an optimist would have called them working engines. By now the Colonel was dead and his former assistant W. H. Austen was in charge. The Southern Railway had managed to avoid being saddled with the KESR at the 1923 Grouping and it was one of the Stephens lines that retained an impecunious independence. In 1932 Rolvenden workshop performed one of its little miracles, managing to salvage or repair enough parts from the two near-derelicts to make one working locomotive. It took *Bodiam's* identity, as the contributor of the most parts, including the frames, which traditionally carry a locomotive's identity.

Bodiam (now nameless) remained at work on the KESR, helped out by class sisters and other engines borrowed from the Southern, until the line was nationalised in 1948. BR closed the line to passengers almost as soon as was decently

possible but it remained one of the few places where 'Terriers' could be seen at work for most of the 1950s.

Continuing the story of the class as a whole, the next set of sales were perhaps the most unlikely. Three 'Terriers' were sold to other main line companies: *Newington* and *Clapham* to the London & South Western in 1903, and *Waddon* to the South Eastern & Chatham in 1904.

The LSWR was looking for small and light engines to operate the recently completed Axminster to Lyme Regis branch. Having nothing that seemed suitable, it chose to buy a pair of 'Terriers' rather than design and build new engines. One reason might be that the Locomotive Department was headed by the legendary Dugald Drummond, who had been Stroudley's assistant at Brighton when the 'Terriers' were produced. While history does not suggest that he was a man given to sentiment, he knew a good design when he saw one and clearly thought that the 'Terriers' were ideal for the job.

Unusually for Drummond, he was wrong. The 12ft fixed wheelbase was too long to take kindly to the branch's sharp curves and the result was unacceptable sidewear; and while they could cope with the normal traffic, the line's steep gradients meant that they had little or nothing in reserve at the busiest times. Within a few years they had been replaced by Adams 0-4-4T 'O2s', which were still not ideal, but were bigger and yet had a shorter fixed wheelbase.

It was not a total disaster for *Newington* and

Above:
In 1923, with everything still in pre-Grouping colours, *Peckham*/IWC No 10 is seen near Smallbrook Junction with a coal train. Light goods work was an important part of 'Terrier' duties on the island.
Isle of Wight Steam Railway Collection

Below:
No W11 (*Brighton*) runs into Newport with a train from Freshwater, formed of LBSC Billinton four-wheelers, in the early SR period. One of the IWC's Beyer Peacock 2-4-0Ts is in the background.
Isle of Wight Steam Railway Collection

Clapham, by now LSWR Nos 734 and 735. Both were found plenty of light duties to keep them busy and were sufficiently useful to be given new boilers and cylinders in 1912, the boilers being typical Drummond items with direct-loaded safety valves on the dome. No 735 was soon to settle down to a useful career on the Lee-on-the-Solent branch, not all that far from her Brighton sisters on the Hayling Island line. No 734 was to have a more varied future.

In 1913 the Freshwater, Yarmouth & Newport, the smallest railway company on the Isle of Wight, fell out spectacularly with its neighbour, the Isle of Wight Central. As the IWC had been operating the FYN's services, with IWC stock, this posed a rather serious problem for the FYN. It had to find locomotives and stock quickly and — of course — cheaply. The LSWR offered to hire No 734, an offer which was gratefully accepted. In 1914 the FYN was able to buy the loco (helped by the LSWR agreeing to hire-purchase terms) and it became FYN No 2. In due course it joined the Southern Railway fleet as No 2 in the Isle of Wight list, later being renumbered into the island's 'Terrier' series as W8 and being named *Freshwater*.

Waddon was bought by the SECR to operate the Sheppey Light Railway; again, a one-off purchase was presumably much cheaper than building a single locomotive from scratch. The railway had been built by Col Stephens but was operated by

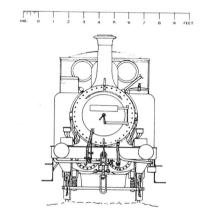

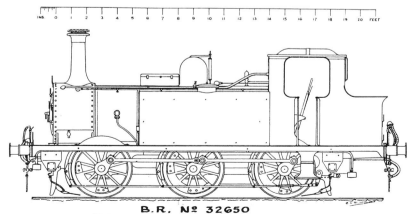

B. R. Nº 32650
(EXTENDED BALANCE WEIGHTS ARE CORRECT FOR PREVIOUS ISLE OF WIGHT USE **NOT** FOR BRITISH RAILWAYS.)

the SECR; whether Stephens recommended a 'Terrier' or whether CME Harry Wainwright made up his own mind cannot now be said.

It is easy to picture the gloating delight in Brighton Works as *Waddon* was given an overhaul to ensure that it was in a fit state for dispatch to the hated rivals at Ashford. Whatever the realities, the shop-floor view would be that that lot on the SECR were reduced to buying Brighton's cast-offs to work its new branch lines. Conceit vanished like a burst balloon when, within a week of entering SECR service, *Waddon* made known its opinion of the move by breaking a crank axle! Red faces must have been in evidence as Brighton hurriedly forwarded a replacement axle — free of charge.

Despite the bad start, the move proved successful for the SLR and it saved *Waddon*, which over the next 50-odd years had several narrow escapes. As No 751 it was reboilered in 1910 with a typical Wainwright product, which lasted until it received a standard 'A1X' boiler in 1937. It put in several years on the SLR and when displaced made itself generally useful as a shed pilot and dock shunter at various locations.

Sales of 'Terriers' halted in 1906, the result of the successful motor train experiment. The remaining fleet was needed and it was not until 1918 that history repeated itself; train weights were increasing and the 'Terriers' were being displaced by bigger engines. Five went in that year for military service: *Southdown*, *Millwall*, *Minories*, *Beulah* and *Earlswood*. In 1920 *Brixton* was sold for industrial use, finishing up at a colliery near Chesterfield. *Deptford* and *Shadwell* were sold in 1919 and 1920 respectively, to the Edge Hill Light Railway, another Col Stephens line.

The five that were 'called up' (the government request for surplus locomotives for military use fell not far short of requisition) entered Admiralty service, initially in Scotland. Their National Service was comparatively brief and most seem to have been laid aside in 1919/20. Col Stephens bought three of them, this time for the Shropshire & Montgomeryshire, an 18-mile line which eked out an existence in the Welsh Marches west of Shrewsbury. *Beulah* arrived in 1921, *Millwall* and *Earlswood* joining it in 1923. *Minories* made its way to Chatham Dockyard, where it survived into the early 1930s, and *Southdown* was scrapped in Scotland in the early 1920s.

Beulah, *Millwall* and *Earlswood* became Nos 7-9 *Hecate*, *Dido* and *Daphne* on the S&M (Col Stephens had a penchant for mythological names). They played a major part in keeping the line's scant passenger traffic and rather healthier goods traffic on the move for nearly a decade. *Hecate* and *Dido* were withdrawn in 1930 and scrapped in 1934, their best parts having been removed to patch up *Daphne*. By then the S&M had scraped together enough to buy three ex-LNWR 0-6-0s which were rather more suitable for the length of run and the traffic on offer, and in much better order than the run-down relics the 'Terriers' had become. *Daphne* lasted as a reserve engine until the late 1930s and in a surprising twist of fate was sold back to the Southern in 1939; not for return to traffic though. It sat at

Below:
Carisbrooke at Freshwater in August 1936, waiting to leave with a Newport train. Four bogie coaches would be quite taxing for a 'Terrier' on the undulating FYN line. *H. F. Wheeller/R. C. Riley Collection*

Eastleigh for another 10 years as a source of spares for the SR's 'Terrier' fleet until it formally ceased to exist with the scrapping of its frames and a few other parts in 1949.

Deptford and *Shadwell* had a rather curious time in the Colonel's hands. The Edge Hill Light Railway was a mineral line running two miles from Burton Dassett (on the Stratford-upon-Avon & Midland Junction Railway) to the foot of a rope-worked incline that brought ironstone down from a quarry. The line opened in 1920 and closed when the ironstone was exhausted five years later, which suggests a serious miscalculation on the part of the promoters. The 'Terriers', with a Manning Wardle 0-4-0ST, shunted the yards and operated the adhesion section of the line.

When the EHLR closed in 1925, everything was just left where it stood, as if the staff went home one night and never bothered to come in again. Thirteen years later the engines and wagons were reported as still standing there, more derelict and decrepit but otherwise largely as they had been left. The site was cleared and the locos and stock scrapped only in 1947.

The puzzle is why the two 'Terriers' were simply left there. Stephens was always short of locomotives for his various lines and in view of his connections with the Edge Hill, it is curious that the pair were abandoned, rather than being moved to another part of his empire. Possibly they were so run down after five years on the EHLR that they were beyond redemption for passenger service.

Above:
One of the last two 'Terriers' to leave the island, *Carisbrooke* was repainted in full Bulleid malachite green livery as the IoW system spruced up for a revival of the tourist trade at the end of the war. The only 'Terrier' to carry the livery, the result was rather garish on so small a machine. *G. L. Nicholson/ R. C. Riley Collection*

Below:
Gipsyhill looks rather plain in WC&PR colours, following its sale to that line in 1925. It has however gained *Portishead* nameplates. *H. C. Casserley/ R. C. Riley Collection*

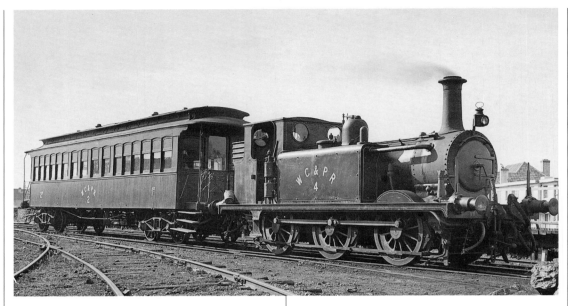

The Grouping and Afterwards

Formed on 1 January 1923, the Southern Railway inherited 16 'Terriers' from the LBSC. Two of them, *Tulsehill* and *Boxhill*, were still 'A1s' and had been transferred from the capital list to the Service Department stock. *Clapham* and *Waddon* rejoined the list from the LSWR and SECR; *Blackwall*, *Peckham*, *Brighton* and *Crowborough* (the latter two being 'A1Xs') were contributed by the IWCR and the FYN's *Newington* rejoined the fold. *Fenchurch* joined the SR list in 1927.

In all then, the SR inherited 24 'Terriers' — practically half the original fleet — and although some did not last very long, half that number were to outlast the new company, passing to British Railways ownership in 1948.

With less work than ever remaining for the class, the new company soon withdrew several, though not all were scrapped; a lucky few were stored and later reinstated. Their last few regular push-pull duties were being taken over by larger engines (mainly Stroudley 'D1' 0-4-2Ts) and finally ended in 1928. That left the class with two main public areas of activity, Hayling Island and the Isle of Wight, the rest being available for various odd jobs around the system, mainly engine shed and works pilot and shunting duties — and of course Newhaven.

Brighton Works, having got its claws on *Boxhill*, clung on to it grimly. By 1925 it was the last 'A1' and the Works would barely let it out of its sight, even in the years in the 1930s when the Works was practically mothballed. It fought

Above:
Ashtead had to be content with plain No 4 when it arrived on the WC&P in 1937. It is seen with one of the line's American-style coaches, a cancelled order for Argentina which the WC&P bought at a bargain price. The curved lettering on the tankside has a certain house-style similarity with that on the KESR of the same period. *Lens of Sutton/R. C. Riley Collection*

Boxhill's case hard and was rewarded in 1946 when the SR recognised that the engine was an important historic artifact as well as a useful works shunter. *Boxhill* was duly reclassified as a retained relic, the first step of its journey to its current home in the National Railway Museum as part of the National Collection. Brighton Works was allowed to return the engine to close to original condition and livery and in 1947 its working career came to an end, future appearances being at exhibitions until it entered Clapham Transport Museum in 1961.

Having several surplus 'Terriers', the SR was in a position to hire one out from time to time (the KESR became a regular customer) and also to augment the position on the Isle of Wight. *Carisbrooke* (*Blackwall*) was withdrawn, worn out, in 1926 but over the next three years three more were sent across, *Wonersh*, *Knowle* and *Whitechapel*, which became *Carisbrooke*, *Bembridge* and *Fishbourne*. The early 1930s were the heyday of the 'Island Terriers', with seven in service, mainly working the Freshwater, Ventnor West and Bembridge passenger services and light goods traffic over much of the system. But the arrival of four Stroudley 'E1' 0-6-0Ts for goods traffic, the delivery of more 'O2s' as the system's standard class and the upgrading of the branches so that they could cope with these heavier engines, saw the need for 'Terriers' decline sharply. *Cowes* (*Peckham*) and *Ventnor* (*Crowborough*) returned in 1936 and were withdrawn; *Bembridge* and *Fishbourne* returned at the same time but re-entered mainland service. The last three remained until after the war, when the key reason for replacing them with 'O2s' was that they were non-standard to the island fleet and caused a logistics problem in keeping Ryde Works stocked with spares.

These years also saw the last two sales of 'Terriers' (until 1960), being the pair that went to the Weston, Clevedon & Portishead Railway. *Gipsyhill* was sold in 1925, to ease the crisis caused when several of the WC&P's fleet of improbable relics saw fit to expire at once. It was — of course — another of Col Stephens's lines and the new arrival, as No 2 *Portishead*, eased things considerably. So much so that in 1937, when another motive power crisis hit the line, W. H. Austen persuaded the SR to part with another 'Terrier' and *Ashtead* became WC&P No 4.

At a time when nearly all the other Col Stephens 'Terriers' were sinking softly into oblivion, this pair had a curious fate, including, of all things, ownership by the Great Western Railway. World War 2 finally finished off the struggling line; it closed in 1940 and the Great Western bought the surviving assets, of which the 'Terriers' were the only mechanical ones really worth having. They were dispatched to Swindon Works, entered the GWR stock book as Nos 5 and 6[4] and were given overhauls in 1941.

Things would have been very different a few years either way but these were the war years and any reasonably usable locos were not being thrown away. Collett, the great Swindoniser of imported engines of other traditions, was dead, or heaven knows what they might have emerged looking like. Under his successor, Hawksworth's, gentler hand, the pair emerged little changed, in GWR unlined green livery with tankside roundels and cast numberplates on the bunkers but easily recognisable as 'Terriers'.

Initially used for dock shunting at Bristol, they did not prove popular; No 6 lasted less than two years before withdrawal and was stored until being scrapped in 1948, while No 5 ended up as a shed pilot at Newton Abbot. Again it seems not to have been liked (the trouble was probably that

Below:
Gipsyhill must surely win the prize for the most unlikely of all 'Terrier' liveries! It is seen stored in the stock shed at Swindon in 1952, following its brief career as a Great Western engine. One of the few changes made by Swindon was to lower the boiler handrail.
R. C. Riley

[4]Nos 1-4 were the old Corris Railway engines and 7-9 were the Vale of Rheidol fleet, so the WCPR pair were among some pretty interesting company at the bottom end of the GWR number list.

they were alien machines to men brought up in an unbroken tradition stretching back to the days of Daniel Gooch) and by 1950 was back at Swindon, where it languished in a dark corner until withdrawn and scrapped in 1954.

Back home on the Southern, the 'Terriers' kept their hold on the Hayling Island line and their other, more scattered duties. Class numbers slowly declined, the crucial factor being spare parts. A 'Terrier' would be withdrawn when something went seriously wrong with it and would then slowly disintegrate at Eastleigh as parts were removed to keep the others going. Finally its remains would be scrapped and the next time a 'Terrier' had a major fault the process would be repeated. This perhaps over-simplifies what happened but summarises the policy of the Locomotive Department. So long as the 'Terriers' were operable, work could be found for them, but resources were not available for major rebuilds.

There was a curious little sideline to 'Terrier' life in 1946 when *Whitechapel* was converted to oil burning for a few months. This was a result of the government's urgent 'export drive' of the time; overseas markets had been found for coal and some bright spark in the civil service had the brainwave that if railway engines were converted to burn oil, more coal would be available for export. The ministers concerned swallowed this hook, line and sinker, and the railways were requested (with nationalisation being prepared, they could hardly refuse) to begin trials with a view to a major conversion programme. The SR converted a 'King Arthur' and *Whitechapel*, whose oil fire obliged by producing a reasonable amount of heat and large clouds of smelly, black smoke. A great deal of time and trouble went into trying to make the thing work before some success was achieved, and the major conversion scheme was just about to get under way when it dawned on the government that the money made by exporting the extra coal was more than cancelled out by the cost of buying imported oil. The whole project was quickly and quietly abandoned — a textbook example of what can happen when governments have ideas about running railways.

By the 1940s the 'Terriers' were the oldest engines owned by the SR and the smallest in regular passenger service. To the public at large, they were starting to acquire a certain curiosity value. In 1947, at the end of the SR's existence, it still had 14 'Terriers' on its books to hand on to British Railways.

Right:
Swindon Works produced a set of drawings for the WC&P pair. This trace of the basic outline, with updated information, was taken in 1950.
R. C. Riley Collection

Below:
Members of the three classes the SR standardised on for the Isle of Wight line up at Newport: 'E1' No 4 *Wroxall* (LBSC *Gournay*), 'A1X' No 13 *Carisbrooke* (*Wonersh*) and 'O2' No 27 *Merstone*.
S. W. Baker/R. C. Riley Collection

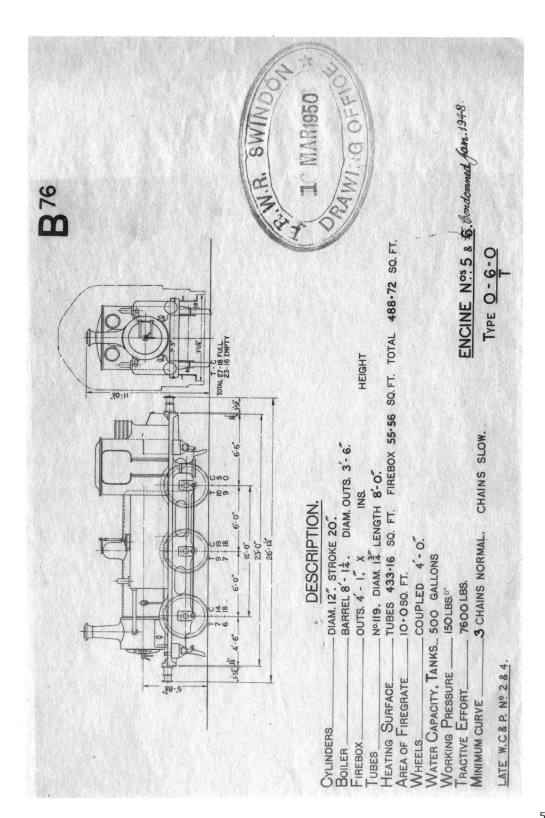

B 76

G.W.R. SWINDON ★ DRAWING OFFICE
1c MAR 1950

DESCRIPTION.

CYLINDERS ———— DIAM. 12". STROKE 20".
BOILER ————— BARREL 8'-1¼. DIAM. OUTS. 3'-6".
FIREBOX ————— OUTS. 4'-1". X INS.
TUBES ————— Nº 119. DIAM. 1⅜" LENGTH 8'-0".
HEATING SURFACE — TUBES 433·16 SQ. FT. FIREBOX 55·56 SQ. FT. TOTAL 488·72 SQ. FT.
AREA OF FIREGRATE — 10·0 SQ. FT.
WHEELS ————— COUPLED 4'-0".
WATER CAPACITY, TANKS 500 GALLONS
WORKING PRESSURE — 150 LBS.☐
TRACTIVE EFFORT —— 7600 LBS.
MINIMUM CURVE ——— 3 CHAINS NORMAL. CHAINS SLOW.

LATE W.C & P. Nº 2 & 4.

ENGINE Nºs 5 & 6. *Condemned Jan. 1948.*

TYPE O-6-O / T

HEIGHT

TOTAL 27·18 FULL
23·16 EMPTY

Top:
Waddon and *Whitechapel*, which formed Lancing
Works' rather generous allocation of 'Terrier' power in
late SR/early BR days, are seen together in the Works
yard. *Waddon* is by now in its hybrid 'A1/A1X' state,
plus Drummond chimney. The different lettering styles
of an engine put through Works for departmental duties
and one transferred straight from the traffic fleet make
an interesting comparison. Lancing was a 'Terrier'
haunt continuously from 1913 to the last days of the
class. *R. H. Tunstall/R. C. Riley Collection*

Above:
Whitechapel, Knowle and *Peckham* (IoW *Fishbourne,
Bembridge* and *Cowes*) stand dumped at Eastleigh
following their withdrawal and return from the island in
1936. *Peckham* was duly scrapped but the other two
were reinstated and both have survived in active
preservation. *Lens of Sutton/
Klaus Marx Collection*

Withdrawals (SR)

NO.	NAME	WITHDRAWN	FATE
B642	*Tulsehill*	1925	Scrapped [had been reinstated 1923]
B643	*Gipsyhill*	1925	Sold, WCPR
B655	*Stepney*	1925	Reinstated, 1927
B663	*Preston*	1925	Scrapped
B677	*Wonersh*	1925	Reinstated (IoW), 1927
B680	*Bookham*	1925	Scrapped
W9	*Carisbrooke [Blackwall]*	1926	Scrapped
A751	*Waddon*	1932	Service Dept
735	*Clapham*	1936	Scrapped
W10	*Cowes [Peckham]*	1936	Scrapped (1949)
W12	*Ventnor [Crowborough]*	1936	Scrapped (1949)
2650	*Whitechapel*	1937	Service Dept
2653	*Ashtead*	1937	Sold, WCPR
2635	*Morden*	1946	Service Dept
380S	*Boxhill*	1947	Officially preserved

List is in original LBSC numerical order for each year

Above:
Two Stroudley yellow 'Terriers' together again at Brighton Works in 1947. *Boxhill*, restored to nearly original condition and officially withdrawn for preservation, stands next to *Morden* which took over its duties. Whether through accidental or deliberate over-ordering, the Works had enough yellow paint left after completing *Boxhill* to be able to repaint *Morden* too; it was to become something of a celebrity, keeping the Stroudley livery and in demand for special appearances for the remainder of its career.
R. C. Riley Collection

CHAPTER FIVE

BR's Oldest Engines

British Railways came into existence on 1 January 1948, the result of nationalising the Big Four railway companies and the various minnows that had escaped the 1923 Grouping. Of the huge and varied stock of locomotives it inherited, the 'Terriers' were among the oldest; just a handful of ex-LMS classes, with a few engines left in each, were of greater age and they were soon to be withdrawn.

BR inherited 16 'Terriers': 14 from the Southern, the lonely GWR No 5 and the Kent & East Sussex's *Bodiam*. No 5 would never work again but the other 15 continued to perform their usual duties. The last pair left the Isle of Wight in 1949, ending a 50-year association with that system, leaving Hayling Island and the KESR as the last passenger strongholds.

As a passenger line the KESR was on its last legs and although the arrival of BR resulted in a considerable improvement in terms of rolling stock used, this was not enough to revive the trade to anything like a financially acceptable level. For several years Rolvenden shed continued to be the home of two or three 'Terriers' based there, including *Bodiam*, now nameless and renumbered from No 3 to 32670 but still for a

while carrying its KESR green livery. But in January 1954 the line was closed to passengers and abandoned completely north of Tenterden, leaving the Robertsbridge-Tenterden section as a goods-only line. The line's 'Terriers' were left in charge, their light weight meaning that repairs to the very tired permanent way and underline structures could be kept to a minimum. They were relocated to St Leonards MPD and had a fairly restful career handling what KESR traffic remained plus any other odd jobs that came their way.

In the early autumn the KESR would come to life, justifying for a few weeks the provision of two 'Terriers' plus a spare. This was harvest-time in the hop gardens that then filled much of the valley from Robertsbridge to Rolvenden and special trains, often needing two 'Terriers', brought hop-pickers from London's East End to the KESR's little stations. This was a social phenomenon of the time, when many East Enders had holidays but no money to do much with them, so went on working breaks to the hop gardens, which needed a large but brief influx of labour. Luckily for the brewing industry, better pay and paid holidays in the East End, which

Left:
The first year of BR was *Carisbrooke's* last full year of the Isle of Wight. It is seen at Merstone in September 1948, its SR ownership painted out with a malachite patch and 'British Railways', in similar style, in its place.
Isle of Wight Steam Railway Collection

Above:
Renumbered but otherwise still in SR Bulleid livery, *Knowle* is seen at Eastbourne in a somewhat battered state, on its way to Brighton Works following its derailment and fall into a swamp at Wittersham Road in March 1949. *S. E. Teasdale/ R. C. Riley Collection*

Right:
Following repairs, *Knowle* is seen stored at Ashford in October 1949, partially repainted into the new lined black livery; apparently transfers for the number but not the new BR motif were available at the time.*R. H. Tunstall/Ian Allan Library*

killed off hop-picking 'holidays', coincided with the arrival of hop picking machines and other developments, otherwise the price of beer would have gone even further through the roof than it has! But the end of the hop pickers' specials was one more nail in the KESR's coffin. The specials last ran in 1958, the year in which the goods service was handed over to 204hp Drewry diesel 0-6-0s (a move which did not save the line, for it closed in 1961).

The loss of the KESR left the 4¹/₂-mile Hayling Island branch as the last passenger service stronghold of the 'Terriers'. But this line, on which the class had had a stranglehold since the 1890s, was a very different kettle of fish. Even in the 1950s it was busy, with a respectable level of service, and if not prosperous enough to justify capital investment, it jogged along generally on the black side of the balance sheet. Running south

from Havant, over the timber trestle Langstone Harbour Bridge, it followed the west edge of Hayling Island to a terminus near its Channel coast. With two intermediate stations, the line was easily graded or level throughout and a 'Terrier' could easily manage three or four coaches. South Hayling was a fair-sized community and still at the time a well-patronised holiday resort; the alternatives to the train were a passenger ferry to the 'wrong end' of Portsmouth, or by car over a toll bridge to Havant. On summer Saturdays the line was bustling, with the service needing three 'Terriers' plus a fourth standing by at Fratton for when anyone ran short of coal. It kept the 'Terriers' in the public eye and even passengers not going to Hayling Island might well notice, as their state-of-the-art Southern Electric unit swept into Havant on a Portsmouth Direct service or a coast trip to Brighton, the diminutive, elderly tank engine standing on a few old coaches in the bay platform, and marvel that such an anachronism was still at work.

It could not last of course; growth of car ownership and a change in holiday habits, combined with local road improvements including an upgrade of the Langstone road bridge, hit the branch's traffic figures. The rail bridge would soon need major repairs and the 'Terriers' could not last much longer on a BR now committed to abolishing steam traction. BR faced the choice of heavy investment on a line which might soon become unprofitable, or closure. By the early 1960s it was understood that the Hayling Island branch was living on borrowed time.

So were the 'Terriers', although their numbers had diminished by only a few in BR days. The class were also well maintained, which caused some surprise among commentators but made sense for engines which not only had sole charge of a branch line but which also had to run fast along an electrified main line to reach it from their MPD. Regular visits to Eastleigh Works (which took over when Brighton finally closed in 1959) continued until 1962, one surprise being that *Fenchurch* visited for major repairs to the back end, including a partly renewed inner firebox, after a shunting incident with a diesel at

Newhaven in 1962. *Fenchurch* came off worse, its rear drawbar being pushed forward and through the firebox plates. It was the last 'Terrier' to receive a heavy repair on BR; by now, with the class known to be nearing the end, it was surprising that it was not withdrawn, as *Wonersh* had been after a shunting mishap in 1959. But it has been said that *Fenchurch* is a lucky engine. By this stage it had been unique for some years as the last of the class to retain the original small bunker without coal rails being fitted to increase its capacity, which probably explains why its stints on Hayling Island duties were rare and brief.

In late 1959 Fratton MPD closed and the 'Terriers' were transferred to Eastleigh but their old home remained a stabling point, where the branch engine would berth overnight. Brisk runs along the Eastleigh-Fareham line became more common but not a daily occurrence.

Enthusiast interest remained as high as ever and with even the national media taking an interest in 'Britain's oldest steam engines' (if, that is, in true journalistic style you ignore all the ones which do not fit the story!), public interest was remarkably high too — higher than it had been when the 'Terriers' first appeared some 90 years earlier. Events had, so to speak, been holding their breath for some years but in early 1963 things began to happen with a flurry.

Above:
The KESR was one of the last lines where mixed trains were commonplace. *Stepney* brings one such into Rolvenden on 7 November 1953. *Colin Hogg*

Left:
On the last day of passenger services, 2 January 1954, *Stepney* passes Cranbrook Road Crossing on Tenterden Bank with the 12.20 from Robertsbridge. *Colin Hogg*

Below left:
Fenchurch is seen on the KESR with a hop-pickers' train at Northiam on 12 September 1953. *Colin Hogg*

Bottom left:
Fenchurch is seen near Wittersham Road with the Tenterden-Robertsbridge goods on 13 September 1958. The line was now officially diesel-worked but the 'Terrier' was held at Ashford as a standby pending the arrival of enough diesels to displace it completely, and had moved, with *Martello*, to St Leonards for the hop-pickers' specials, just in time for No 11223 to go to Ashford for repairs, leaving the veterans in charge for a few days. *J. J. Smith/R. C. Riley Collection*

Opposite page:
Fenchurch and *Knowle* double-head the 5.14 Bexhill West-Bodiam empty stock near Crowhurst on 23 September 1956, to form that evening's hop pickers' special off the KESR. *Fenchurch* was by now in a peripatetic phase, having loosened its ties with Newhaven. *Colin Hogg*

Right:
At Brighton in July 1948, *Fulham* shows evidence of a quick partial repaint and new identity.
H. C. Casserley/ K. Marx Collection

Below right:
The transfer of trains on and off the KESR line would bring a brief flurry of activity to Robertsbridge, with engines needing servicing, running round, stock being shunted and other aspects of junction life. *Fenchurch* and *Knowle* are seen by the water tower, with the KESR line curving off on the extreme right. *Mike Esau*

Below:
Enthusiasts' specials also became a feature of the latter days of the KESR. *Fenchurch* heads away from West St Leonards with the empty stock for a special on 12 April 1958.
Colin Hogg

Above right:
Passengers disembark to photograph or explore as *Bodiam* waits with an enthusiasts' special at Rolvenden. Sadly, such a carefree and unregimented approach to such trains is a thing of the past. *Mike Esau*

Below right:
Final closure is imminent as *Martello* heads the LCGB's 'South Eastern Ltd' past one of the hop gardens that once characterised the Rother Valley, between Bodiam and Northiam on 11 June 1961. *Bodiam* is pushing at the rear of the train, which is too long for the line's loops. *Mike Esau*

Closure of the Hayling Island branch was set for November. Before that, the final departmental duties were taken over by other locomotives and the other 'Terrier' stronghold, Newhaven West Quay, was closed. With the crossing of the venerable Newhaven swing bridge eliminated, other motive power could deal with what little shunting remained at Newhaven.

After a few early withdrawals, BR had kept the rest of the class in service and not until 1959 were any more to be declared redundant. One was to go as surplus in 1960; this was when events took a new turn and the infant Bluebell Railway approached BR to buy a 'Terrier'. With buyer and seller both willing, Stepney was withdrawn and went to its new home in May 1960. A second approach a few months later brought the response that no further 'Terriers' could be spared!

That situation lasted until 1962, when Waddon, which had spent most of the past 30 years minding its own business as Lancing Works shunter, was presented to the Canadian Railway Historical Association — though it carried on with its Lancing duties for a while before an overhaul and shipping to Canada were arranged. Waddon had had a series of narrow escapes, having been stored pending withdrawal in the late 1920s, reprieved to act as a stationary boiler (which was normally the last rite before a death sentence was carried out), then overhauled and sent to Lancing Works, a job which really only needed one engine but the Works managed to hang on to two 'Terriers' for years. After its 1932 overhaul Waddon was a hybrid, effectively an 'A1' with an 'A1X' boiler and it was returned to near-Stroudley condition for Canada, the only visual give-away being the minor one of the dome.

In 1963 BR set about reducing the class to the minimum needed for the last few months of the Hayling Island line. Morden and Sutton were withdrawn and scrapped, as was Cheam, which had been a Service Department engine for 10 years. This left just seven: Brighton, Newington, Whitechapel, Martello, Poplar, Fenchurch and Knowle. But

already interest in the 'Terriers' was taking the positive form of approaches to BR asking for a price and somebody realised that scrapping a 'Terrier' was the equivalent of chopping a stack of £5 notes into small pieces. The scrappings stopped abruptly (though just too late for Morden and Sutton, which were cut up in September) and Brighton and Knowle, withdrawn before the end of the Hayling Island branch, were placed in store.

The final trains on the Hayling Island branch ran on the first weekend in November, well supported in the traditional way of such events. The last day of public service, Saturday 2 November, was worked by Whitechapel, Martello and Poplar. On Sunday 3rd, Poplar and Fenchurch worked specials, including the Locomotive Club of Great Britain's five-coach 'Hayling Farewell', which the veterans topped and tailed. So the final day's workings were in the hands of BR's longest-serving locomotives. When Fenchurch's fire was drawn that evening, it was the last 'Terrier' in service, just as, 91 years earlier, it had been the first.

Withdrawals (BR)

NO.	NAME	WITHDRAWN	FATE
6	Ashtead	1948	Scrapped (Swindon)
5	Gipsyhill	1950	Scrapped (Swindon)
32644	Fulham	1951	Scrapped
32647	Cheapside	1951	Scrapped
32659	Cheam	1953	To Service Dept (scrapped 1963)
32677	Wonersh	1959	Scrapped
32655	Stepney	1960	Sold, Bluebell Railway
DS680	Waddon	1962	Presented to Canadian Railway Historical Assn
32635	Morden	1963	Scrapped [had been reinstated 1959]
32640	Brighton	1963	Sold, Butlins
32646	Newington	1963	Sold, Saddler Railcar Co
32650	Whitechapel	1963	Sold, Borough of Sutton [had been reinstated 1953]
32661	Sutton	1963	Scrapped
32662	Martello	1963	Sold, Butlins
32670	Poplar	1963	Sold, KESR Pres Soc
32636	Fenchurch	1963	Sold, Bluebell Railway
32678	Knowle	1963	Sold, Butlins

List is in original LBSC numerical order for each year.

Above left:
Knowle stands in the KESR platform at Robertsbridge with a hop-pickers' special in September 1958.
Mike Esau

Left:
Bodiam waits to leave Robertsbridge with the stock of a hop-pickers' special bound for St Leonards.
Mike Esau

Above:
Bodiam gets plenty of attention at Cranbrook Road Crossing, with the 'South Eastern Ltd'. This, like several other KESR level crossings, was unprotected.
Mike Esau

Below:
Sutton is seen on its way from Havant to Langstone and Hayling Island on 1 September 1951.
Brian Morrison

Left:
A somewhat grubby *Stepney*, its scorched smokebox door hinting at over-work, stands at Havant on 1 September 1951, waiting to work a train to Hayling Island. *Brian Morrison*

Below:
Newington takes the sharp curve out of Havant and away from the main lines. *Mike Esau*

Right
Sutton heads a train for Hayling Island across Langstone Bridge, the line's most notable feature and its Achilles' heel. The engine is fitted with the spark arrester that was a typical feature of the line in its last years. *Mike Esau*

Above left:
Sutton rolls into Hayling Island…
Mike Esau

Left:
… and rests at the end of yet another journey down
the branch. *Mike Esau*

Top:
Whitechapel pauses at North Hayling on its way to the
terminus in August 1962. *J. Scrace*

Above:
Fenchurch heads across Newhaven swing bridge
towards the main line yard in July 1950.
R. C. Riley

Above left:
Inside Newhaven shed, *Newington* and *Fenchurch* (the former, unusually, with coal rails extending its IoW bunker) share space with 'E4' No 23475 (*Partridge Green*) on 2 October 1954.
Brian Morrison

Left:
Knowle backs across the swing bridge, heading for the West Quay, on 26 July 1963.
E. Wilmshurst

Top:
On 10 August 1963, the last day of operating the West Quay lines, *Knowle* poses for the cameras, having rounded up a few last wagons near the limits of the sidings. *R. C. Riley*

Above:
Later that day, *Knowle* crosses the swing bridge with the final train from the West Quay lines.
R. C. Riley

Left:
On 18 August 1963 Newhaven bids a fond farewell to its last 'Terrier' as *Knowle* prepares to leave for Brighton. The shed was to close shortly afterwards. *R. C. Riley*

Above left:
Calls for 'Terriers' to work special trains were becoming more common during the 1950s. On 5 and 19 October 1952 Brighton Atlantic No 32424 *Beachy Head* (soon to be the last of that famous class) worked specials from London to mark the centenary of Brighton Works. *Fenchurch* worked a shuttle service from Brighton to Kemp Town in conjunction, and is seen passing the front of the Atlantic as it propels an ex-LBSC push-pull set past the works. *P. Ransome-Wallis*

Above:
Poplar was the first — and last — 'Terrier' to visit North Kent for many years when in March 1956 it stood in for 'P' No 31178 at Ridham Dock. It is seen here with one of Bowaters' fleet, 0-6-2T *Triumph*. *W. M. J. Jackson/R. C. Riley Collection*

Below:
In its yellow 'Brighton Works' livery, *Morden* was popular for special events. Here it is seen at Whyteleafe South on the Caterham line, heading an SECR Birdcage set on a special to mark the line's centenary in 1956. *Klaus Marx Collection*

Above:
Morden again, this time with a special at Kemp Town. The 'Terrier' is emerging from the tunnel mouth, where the station throat pointwork was squeezed in, while running round its train. *R. C. Riley*

Below:
In October 1962 *Fenchurch* and 'E6' No 32418 run off the London Road Viaduct and approach Brighton station with an RCTS special from Seaford. *R. C. Riley*

Morden, as the Brighton Works 'Terrier', defiantly carried its pre-BR No 377S (as distinct from the politically correct DS377) for some years, rather than have any horrors committed to its Stroudley livery. It is seen quietly awaiting its next job on 2 October 1954. *Brian Morrison*

Below:
On 17 July 1958 *Brighton* is seen at Midhurst, a one-time 'Terrier' haunt, on special duties for the film *Carleton Browne, FO* starring Terry-Thomas. *W. M. J. Jackson/ R. C. Riley Collection*

Top:
Last day of public service on the Hayling Island branch, 2 November 1963. *Whitechapel* is seen near North Hayling, heading for the bridge and Havant. *Mike Esau*

Above:
In 1959, to the surprise of many, *Morden* was returned to capital stock and took up its correct BR number, 32635. However, it retained its yellow livery and 'Brighton Works' legend until withdrawn in 1963. *R. K. Evans*

Above right:
One of *Brighton's* last duties before withdrawal was a stint as shed pilot at Brighton. It is seen there in mid-1963; in contrast with earlier views of the shed, it is the only 'Brighton' engine in sight. The tank-front step and extra handrail were features acquired by some of the Isle of Wight 'Terriers'. The 'Wells Fargo Ltd' graffito on the tool box is down to MPD wit. *R. C. Riley*

Right:
Whitechapel leaves Langstone Bridge with a Havant train on 2 November 1963. The signalbox by the bridge's pivoting section is clearly visible. *Mike Esau*

CHAPTER SIX

New Life in Preservation

I n November 1963 BR had its last seven 'Terriers' stored awaiting possible purchase, as early expressions of interest distilled down into a few serious bidders, and the usual crop of casual time-wasters drifted away once they realised that BR was not giving them away for the price of a bag of chips. In the event, all seven found new owners; the price tag of £750 each does not sound much now but represented a year's pay or more for many people at the time. It was around twice the scrap value but these locomotives were being sold in working order.

There were, of course, the three already preserved, *Boxhill*, *Stepney* and *Waddon*, and their subsequent careers are best reviewed first.

Boxhill, the officially preserved example, was given its 'relic' status in 1946 and when BR was formed in 1948 was one of the early members of what has grown to become the National Collection of railway items. It was one of that small but elite group of locomotives deemed worthy of preservation by the Big Four railway companies; and whereas the LNER and its East Coast predecessors had long shown an interest in saving historic machines and had built up a fairly impressive collection, the other three groups had

been more cavalier about their past.[1] *Boxhill* was quite lucky in fact, for the SR had started to form a historical collection in the 1930s. Had *Boxhill* been withdrawn for preservation 10 years earlier, it would have been sacrificed to the wartime scrap drive, along with *Ryde*, Drummond's *Bug* and the others.

As it was, *Boxhill*, lovingly restored to be the most original of the 'Terriers', went on exhibition at the new and then much acclaimed Museum of British Transport at Clapham in 1961. However, the rapid change which was about to grip Britain's railway industry was accompanied by Galloping Preservation, and within a few years the number of stored relics had far outstripped the capacity of Clapham or anything like it. BR, with various sheds round its system stuffed with stored artifacts, was getting restless. A new, grand,

---

[1]*The Great Western and LMS had real stains on their character in this respect. Both were guilty of scrapping previously preserved engines when they were felt to be getting in the way.*

Right:
Newly restored to its Stroudley finery, *Boxhill* stands outside Brighton Works with a brand-new Bulleid Pacific on 7 June 1947.
Klaus Marx Collection

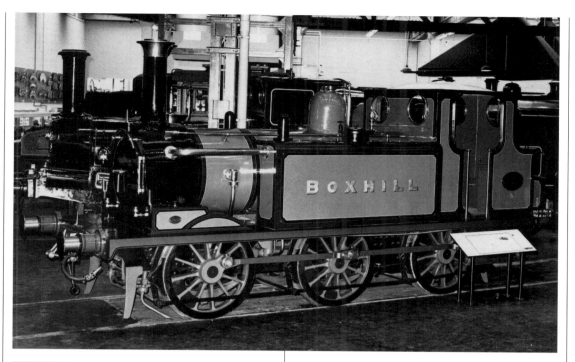

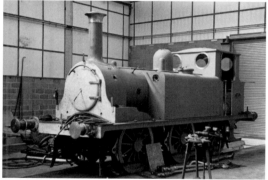

Above:
Boxhill, splendidly presented, in the main hall of the National Railway Museum in 1976. It remains one of the most popular locomotive exhibits. *Brian Morrison*

Left:
In September 1960, *Boxhill* is seen getting the star treatment in the diesel shop at Eastleigh, in preparation for exhibition in the new Transport Museum at Clapham. *A. Swain/R. C. Riley Collection*

National Railway Museum was conceived in London in the early 1970s and born in York in 1975. *Boxhill* took up its place there, rejoining its near contemporary, Stroudley's express engine *Gladstone*, for the first time in many years. The 'Terrier' has since established itself as one of the most popular locomotives in the museum, especially liked by young visitors.

Boxhill has not been in working order since the early 1950s and although it would be perfectly feasible to restore it to steaming condition, this is not likely to happen. The engine is not just a museum exhibit, it is also the datum point, the three dimensional record of the class, against which the others can be compared and to which restorers can turn for first hand historical evidence. With other 'Terriers' to be seen at work, *Boxhill* is too important to risk wearing bits of it out.

Waddon arrived in Canada in early 1963 and has since been at the Canadian Railway Museum at Montreal. She shares the exhibition space not only with some of Canada's finest but with another British exhibit, Gresley's 'A4' Pacific No 60010 *Dominion of Canada*. Also maintained in excellent cosmetic, rather than working, order, Waddon does nothing to disgrace the company it keeps[2].

[2]*Reports in 1998 indicated that* Waddon *was stored out of public view and in need of a repaint.*

Stepney by contrast is a working engine, although the changed needs of the Bluebell Railway have rather pushed the small engines into the background and it has had two long periods out of traffic. After delivery in 1960 in plain black livery, it spent that first season working the two-coach train (the railway's entire stock) with SECR 'P' class 0-6-0T No 31323, the engine that the Bluebell bought because no further 'Terriers' were available.

The choice of a 'Terrier' for the line is easy to explain. The Bluebell Railway was established on a section of former LBSC branch line and the young preservation society included a good number of 'Brighton' enthusiasts. In the late 1950s and early 1960s there were still plenty of people around who could remember the Brighton, and many more who could remember it as the Central Section of the Southern Railway. A Brighton — preferably Stroudley — engine was a *sine qua non*, which narrowed the field down considerably. A 'Terrier' was the obvious choice. So for several years *Stepney* operated the Bluebell Railway's re-creation of a vanishing form of rural transport, while 50 miles away BR was still running an almost identical train between Havant and Hayling Island, at a somewhat lower fare!

Since 1961 *Stepney* has carried Stroudley livery; not strictly correct as it is a Marsh-condition 'A1X' but nobody really minds. It has represented since 1963 the only chance of seeing Stroudley yellow on a working engine and while it will be some years before the Bluebell's project

of a set of varnished wood four-wheel coaches will be complete to make a complementary train, a pretty close second-best will be available in a few years. The Bluebell's set of four 1898-1901 Metropolitan Railway coaches is undergoing a major restoration. They are short-body bogie coaches and are being restored to varnished teak livery. Once back in traffic this unique train, which is within *Stepney's* capacity, will give a good impression of what travel was like on the London suburban lines 100 years ago.

Stepney had not been long at the Bluebell before the Rev Awdry decided to base one of his famous 'Railway Series' books around it and the Bluebell Railway. This unique case of a real engine taking a starring role in a *Thomas* story has proved to be of real benefit to both engine and railway as *Thomas* fever has increased its hold on the youngest generation. Not surprisingly, many people, including some who should know better, think that the railway named *Stepney* after the book character rather than the other way round! It was the children's genuine affection for *Stepney* (the engine gets a fair bit of juvenile fan-mail) that encouraged the railway to overhaul it in the late 1970s and again in the early 1990s, when traffic requirements were really for bigger machines. Let no one say that the *Thomas* books do no good for preservation.

The other seven preserved 'Terriers' are all from the big sell-off of 1964 (in itself another 'Terrier' event unique in railway history). Three went straight into active preservation, the others arrived by more roundabout routes.

Left:
Waddon is craned aboard a cargo vessel for the journey across the Atlantic to Canada in 1963. *British Railways/R. C. Riley Collection*

Right:
The first standard gauge ex-BR steam engine enters active preservation. On 17 May 1960 *Stepney* hurries out of Clayton Tunnel on its run up the main line from Brighton to Copyhold Junction, en route for the Bluebell Railway. Its train comprises the Bluebell's first two passenger coaches. *S. C. Nash*

Right:
The train passes through Ardingly as it nears the end of its journey. *Lens of Sutton/R. C. Riley Collection*

Right:
Still in black for its first season but with its name and number restored, *Stepney* takes water at Sheffield Park before a special working on 3 July 1960. 'P' class No 323 *Bluebell* can just be seen at the rear of the coaches; this train includes the company's entire stock at the time. *R. C. Riley*

Below:
Repainted into Stroudley livery for the 1961 season, *Stepney* stands at Sheffield Park with newly-arrived 'P' No 27 (briefly named *Primrose*) and the historic ex-Metropolitan Ashbury coaches. No 323 brings up the rear. *R. C. Riley*

The two survivors of the first batch found appropriate homes. The Bluebell Railway had been hoping for some time to buy *Fenchurch*, which went on the Society's official Preservation List once it was clear that the railway had enough potential to justify another 'Terrier'. It was also felt that the chance to buy the first 'Terrier' in traffic, the oldest surviving LBSC engine and the oldest engine on BR could not be missed.[3] The timing could hardly have been worse, for the railway had only recently learned that BR was not prepared to continue renting the line; the Bluebell would have to buy it, at an alarmingly high figure, if it wanted to stay in business. With the line purchase fund established as the first priority, raising money to

[3] *Bluebell was then the only active ex-BR standard gauge preserved railway; in buying a second 'Terrier' on the grounds of historic importance, it was not depriving any other line of much-needed motive power.*

Right:
Fenchurch entered service on the Bluebell immediately after arrival. It is seen waiting to leave Horsted Keynes for Sheffield Park in its first summer on the line, 1964; black paint has restored its SR number (on the BR numberplate!) and obliterated the BR emblem. The juice rail is still in place on the old Ardingly platform but the whole station presents a very bare aspect to anyone who knows it today. *R. C. Riley*

Below:
Stepney made several trips back to BR before the Haywards Heath-Horsted Keynes line was closed in late 1963. Here, it and the Bluebell's LSWR Adams radial tank No 488 leave Haywards Heath with a London-Sheffield Park special, one of several through trains run in those easy-going, early days. *S. C. Nash*

buy another engine was seen by many as an unwelcome diversion. But happily the leaders of the railway persisted, and despite the very disappointing result of an attempt to get sponsorship from some of the big businesses on London's Fenchurch Street, the money was found, without apparent harm to the line purchase fund, and *Fenchurch* delivered itself in May 1964, almost the last train movement to take place over the Haywards Heath to Horsted Keynes line.

With the Bluebell now landlocked, *Fenchurch* was unlikely to repeat *Stepney's* exploits of the previous three years, when excursions onto BR's metals had included working a special from Brighton to the Bluebell and back, double-heading with *Birch Grove*, the Bluebell's Billinton 'E4'. However, *Fenchurch* was to get the chance to show off on BR again…

Fenchurch was soon repainted into Newhaven Harbour Co livery, black lined in red, at first

carrying the name on one side and 'Newhaven Harbour Company' on the other, a re-creation of two different times in the loco's past that was adopted in an attempt to please two schools of thought. The 1970s opened with the engine receiving an overhaul in time for its centenary and although it just missed the correct date (in true preservation fashion, unexpected extra work was found to be necessary), it was in steam again in November, when the delayed celebrations were duly held. *Fenchurch* now carried its name on both sides, a style maintained until 1988, shortly before withdrawal for overhaul, when it was turned out in BR lined black.

In 1975 *Fenchurch* had perhaps its finest hour, when it was invited to the 150th anniversary celebrations of the Stockton & Darlington Railway at Shildon. No 'Terrier' had been at the previous big S&D parties, marking the 50th and 100th anniversaries of opening, so *Fenchurch*, mingling with 30 or more steam engines, mostly famous express machines, was chalking up another battle honour to maintain its pecking order in the class.

Many who were there will remember *Fenchurch*, if only for being the engine with the white coal! Reviving an LBSC tradition for engines on extra-special duties, Bluebell Locomotive Foreman Jack Owen whitewashed the contents of the bunker, to the bemusement of many visitors. Members of the support team still recall the surprise of crews of bigger engines at just how much work the 'Terrier' could do. A century on,

Above:
Fenchurch stands between LYR 'Pug' No 51218 and SR Maunsell 'S15' No 841, waiting to run in the cavalcade, the highlight of the 1975 Stockton & Darlington 150 celebrations at Shildon. Note the white coal! *Mike Esau*

Below:
Newly back in traffic after overhaul, *Fenchurch* stands in Sheffield Park with the LBSC Directors' Saloon on 5 November 1972, after the official run to commemorate its centenary. It was the first ever ex-main line engine to achieve and pass 100 years of active service.
Mike Esau

Stroudley's little masterpiece could still impress an audience. Others will remember the long journey back to Sussex with the low loader, which the police insisted had to spend a night stop in a layby partly occupied by travellers, who were practically drooling at the sight of all that non-ferrous metal parked right under their noses!

It was said at the time that there would never again be such a gathering of steam engines in Britain. Five years later that was disproved, when the even grander Liverpool & Manchester Railway 150th anniversary celebrations were held but sadly *Fenchurch* was not invited to that party. Ironically both the Shildon and Bold Colliery sites, where the displays were held, have now vanished, so if there are any 200th anniversary celebrations for these pioneer lines, they will have to take place somewhere else. Hopefully either *Fenchurch* or one of its sisters will be thought worthy of a place in the cavalcade.

Not long after its return to Sussex, *Fenchurch* surprised the workshops with a firebox failure. It was, after all, the newest of all 'Terrier' fireboxes, dating only to that overhaul in 1962. Whether copper quality had declined by 1962, or whether nobody thought that the new box would have to last very long, it was beyond repair and a new one was fitted (a preservation 'first' for the standard gauge) and *Fenchurch* returned to active duty in 1980. It remained in traffic through the decade but was withdrawn in mid-1989 for repairs. When cracks were detected in the wrought-iron wheel centres it became clear that these repairs would be in fact a major rebuild. In early 1999 *Fenchurch* was finally taking shape

again, the new wheels, whose cost had been largely covered by a special appeal, waiting to be fitted. A pattern for a new cylinder block is also being prepared (a joint project between the railways owning operational 'Terriers') but *Fenchurch* is expected to return to traffic with its old block for a while at least. There are more details about this overhaul in Chapter 7.

Poplar found an even more appropriate home, being bought by two members of the Kent & East Sussex Railway Preservation Society for use again on that line. As *Bodiam*, it had been on the line from 1901 to 1958 (losing its name in the 1930s rebuild) and as *Bodiam* it returned home in April 1964. These were early days for the KESR revival and nobody had any idea of the battles ahead or that it would be another 10 years before the line reopened, and then only the first stage. Even now, after 25 years, the reopened section runs only from Tenterden to Northiam, with the three

miles to Bodiam hopefully reopening by 2000 and a distant possibility of rebuilding the officially 'lost' section thence to Robertsbridge.

Bodiam has played a useful role on the revived KESR and although, as at the Bluebell (and the East London line long ago) train loads now commonly exceed the capacity of a 'Terrier', the situation has been saved to a large extent by the popularity of the line's Vintage Train, a set of veteran coaches within the locomotive's limits. Like the other preserved 'Terriers', its history is a combination of periods spent in service interrupted by long gaps awaiting or receiving overhaul. It was in the most recent of these that Bodiam made preservation history. Along with Newington (Freshwater) on the Isle of Wight, it received a brand-new boiler. The two boilers were built at Israel Newtons, Bradford; it was the first

time that a complete new boiler had ever been made for a preserved BR locomotive.

The increasing frequency of boiler failures, as boilers get older, is a feature of the last 20 years of preservation history. There have been occasions when a boiler has had major repairs and been returned to use, only to develop another serious fault within two years. The work and cost of keeping an old boiler in commission are considerable. The alternative, of building a new boiler, had been shied away from as beyond the reach of preservation. Once again, though, the 'Terriers' have shown the way forward, and while their boilers are smaller and simpler than those of almost any other main line engine, there can be no doubt that others will have to follow where they have led. These two 'Terriers' have boilers which it is reasonable to expect will be relatively

Right:
Bodiam rounds Willow Curve on the approach to Rolvenden with a Wittersham Road-Tenterden train on 1 August 1984, its first day of service in BR colours following overhaul.
Brian Morrison

Right:
Recently delivered from BR and not yet renamed, *Whitechapel* stands in the yard at Robertsbridge, with evidence of its BR ownership blotted out and its number shortened back to its LBSC original. It is easy to forget now that back in the early 1960s many enthusiasts regarded the BR steam era as an unfortunate aberration in British railway history.
John Vaughan

Right:
Wearing its first KESR livery, *Sutton* drifts down the sweeping curve at the top of Tenterden Bank with a train for Rolvenden on 3 March 1974, shortly after the line reopened.
D. M. C. Hepburne-Scott/ Rail Archive Stephenson

Left:
Visits by 'Terriers' to other lines are fairly rare events but *Bodiam* went as far as the Didcot Railway Centre in September 1984. The ex-Brighton engine is seen at that shrine to Great Westernry, waiting to back its train onto the demonstration branch line.
Brian Stephenson

Left:
On 26 September 1976, with a headboard to mark its own centenary, *Sutton* rounds Orpins Curve on the approach to Rolvenden, with a train for Newmill Bridge, the then terminus. The first vehicle is GWR railcar No 26. The name and Borough coat of arms are now on a single cast plate.
Brian Stephenson

Left:
Ten years after reopening, and in a third variation of its KESR green livery, *Sutton* descends Tenterden Bank in August 1984. *Brian Stephenson*

Left:
Recalling the traditional way of working the line, the two KESR 'Terriers' together descend Tenterden Bank with a mixed train in October 1984. Tenterden station is visible, upper left of the picture.
Brian Stephenson

Above:
By now repainted into SR colours, with a new nameplate to resemble Isle of Wight appearance, *Sutton* pilots 'P' No 1556 round Orpins Curve at the start of the climb from Rolvenden to Tenterden on 4 June 1990. The headboard commemorates the recent extension of the line from Wittersham Road to Northiam.
Mike Esau

Right:
With its smokebox door showing signs of damage, *Sutton* stands at Wittersham Road after arrival in April 1979. *Brian Morrison*

trouble-free for 20 years. The same cannot be said of any other preserved standard gauge engine.

Not long after *Bodiam*, another 'Terrier' arrived at the KESR, this time *Whitechapel*. It came on loan from the London Borough of Sutton, the result, in a way, of a near miss. In 1963 someone planted in the minds of the councillors of Sutton the thought that a historic engine, the 'Terrier' *Sutton*, still existed and would it not be a good idea for the Borough to buy it, perhaps to make an interesting centrepiece display in the new civic centre?

In the way of such things, it took some time for the purchase of *Sutton* to progress from being a good idea to being approved council policy with the funds available to back it up. By the time the Borough could make an official approach to BR it was early 1964 and poor *Sutton* was well on

the way to being turned into paperclips. However, BR could offer the Borough the almost identical *Whitechapel*. They could always call it *Sutton* and hardly anyone would know better. Would that do instead?

The Borough agreed and duly paid for *Whitechapel*. The new civic centre being by no means ready for a large piece of industrial sculpture, *Whitechapel/Fishbourne/Sutton* was offered on loan to the KESR. It was duly accepted, arrived in late 1964 and was officially renamed in 1966[4]. In 1974 *Sutton* took part in working both the first passenger train on the reopened line and the official reopening train later in the year and

---

[4]It is the only member of the class to have carried three different names.

Above:
Newly restored to its BR guise as No 32650 (and therefore presumably *Whitechapel* once again!), *Sutton* approaches Northiam with the first train of the year, the 10.00 ex-Tenterden on a very frosty 1 January 1993. *Brian Morrison*

Left:
Restored to its later SR appearance, *Freshwater* is seen at Haven Street in September 1986. *Stuart Duddy*

Left:
In 1989 *Freshwater* was repainted in the livery of the FYNR, to celebrate the centenary of the formation of that company. The engine had of course never carried this livery in its current form. *Stuart Duddy*

Above right:
At the head of a fair-sized train for a 'Terrier', *Freshwater* drifts down the grade towards Haven Street with a Smallbrook-Wootton train in August 1993. *Stuart Duddy*

has since, apart from the usual breaks for overhauls, been an active member of the fleet. At first carrying the bright green livery that the KESR adopted for its house style, it was later turned out in SR Maunsell green, looking very like a 1930s Isle of Wight 'Terrier', complete with nameplates — though retaining its *Sutton* identity and carrying its KESR fleet number 10; in its IoW days it was No W9. In 1993, before withdrawal for overhaul, it appeared in BR livery as No 32650, its correct number rather than *Sutton's* No 32661.

The Borough of Sutton's intentions for the engine have changed over the years, partly because the civic centre project did not develop as first intended. It has been content for the engine to remain at the KESR and in 1981 made a 30-year lease agreement with the railway, which gave Tenterden sufficient confidence in the future to spend time and money putting *Sutton* through the workshops.

Newington has had perhaps the strangest career of all that final seven. At the time of its withdrawal, when the Beeching wave of railway closures was nearing its peak, a number of businesses were set up with the idea of reopening some closed lines on a commercial basis. The Sadler Railcar Co was one of these, aiming to convert unremunerative branch lines into a form of what we now call light rail. Its base was at Droxford on the closed Meon Valley line. This company bought *Newington*, ostensibly for shunting and for powering trial runs of the

prototype railcar. In the event, it did little work and in 1966 it was sold again, this time to the Brickwoods Brewery, who installed it on a plinth outside the 'Hayling Billy' public house on Hayling Island, surely one of the largest pub signs ever. Before leaving Droxford it made a special run for Sadlers, and was dispatched by low loader with the remains of the last steaming still in the boiler and firebox.

At Hayling Island it was repainted in Stroudley livery and got its name back, becoming a feature of the area until the late 1970s. By then Brickwoods had been bought by Whitbreads, who were somewhat less convinced about the marketing advantages of *Newington*. Various preservation groups had made enquiries about the locomotive over the years and when the Wight Locomotive Society, the operators of the Isle of Wight Steam Railway, made an approach with an argued case showing their historic and current suitability as a home for *Newington*, the brewery softened. In 1979 Whitbreads donated *Newington* to the railway, a most generous gesture on their part.

So *Newington* returned to the island that had been its base from 1913 to 1949 and the section of track it had often worked over in the 1920s and 1930s. An examination showed that it was in better condition than its class sister *Newport*, which had been back on the island for several years; remarkably good condition in fact, considering its recent history. An all-out effort had the engine restored to running order in a little over a year. It was restored to Southern Railway Maunsell green livery, retaking its identity as No 8 *Freshwater*, an appearance which it has retained apart from a short spell in FYNR pea green in the late 1980s. It has had just two breaks from service, the second of which, 1997/8, saw it fitted with a new boiler, the second of the pair built by Israel Newton's. Now rejuvenated — the railway is delighted with the boiler's performance — it is back in regular service, a vital member of the IWSR's small locomotive stud.

The final three, *Brighton*, *Martello* and *Knowle*, all went to a surprise purchaser in 1964 — Butlins Holiday Camps. Always on the lookout for new attractions, Butlins caught the mood of nostalgia as the steam age drew towards its close and bought in all eight locomotives: the three 'Terriers', an LSWR 'B4' 0-4-0T, three Stanier Pacifics (*Princess Margaret Rose*, *Duchess of*

Hamilton and *Duchess of Sutherland*) and the ex-LMS 4-6-0 *Royal Scot*. Four camps got a large and small engine each; of the 'Terriers', *Brighton* went to Pwllheli, *Martello* to Point of Ayr and *Knowle* to Minehead.

They were placed on open display, painted in quasi-LBSC liveries and for a time attracted a fair bit of attention, not all of it beneficial in the long term. Some of the youngsters at Butlins camps could play decidedly rough! By the late 1960s though, the novelty of plinthed steam engines had worn off and so had much of the paint applied a few years earlier. Butlins, who to their credit took a responsible view of their custody of these relics, began to look for alternative homes. In the early 1970s all eight moved on, handed over to the keeping of the railway preservation movement.

The strongest contender for rehousing *Brighton* had to be the Isle of Wight Steam Railway — after

Right:
In August 1989 During its first season in steam in 26 years, *Brighton/Newport*, turned out as IWC No 11, pilots *Freshwater* as they run round their train at Haven Street. No 11 has been fitted with a replica Wheeler & Hurst chimney, with its distinctive wide top lip.
Stuart Duddy

Below:
Following purchase by Butlins and cosmetic restoration at Eastleigh, *Martello* is seen at an early stage of its journey to Point of Ayr holiday camp, travelling in style behind *Henley Hall* in September 1964.
T. E. Williams/R. C. Riley Collection

Above:
In Bulleid wartime black livery, *Newport* brings a train of four-wheelers into Haven Street in August 1997. *Stuart Duddy*

Left:
Study of *Newport* in IWC livery. *Stuart Duddy*

all, it had spent 45 years on island metals. Happily the railway was able to persuade Butlins of this and the engine left Wales for old haunts in January 1973. First plans were for a cosmetic overhaul to IWCR condition and work started with this in mind; the infant railway did not feel that it had the ability or resources to manage a return to steam. But confidence and competence grow fast together on young preserved railways and sights were soon set higher. Only when it dismantled *Brighton* did the railway realise the scale of the task as it assessed the deterioration that had occurred since 1963. Still, they plodded on, breaking off to restore *Newington* on the way, and *Brighton* finally emerged in steam, in its guise as IWCR No 11, in 1989. To add to its island character it has been fitted with a replica of the chimney, cast locally by Wheeler & Hurst, that adorned the IWCR 'Terriers' when their originals wore out. It has a distinctive very wide top lip.

The engine has spent most of the 1990s in IWCR guise but in 1997 was turned out, for a change, in the Bulleid-era SR black livery with Sunshine lettering and its island name *Newport*. Only one island 'Terrier', *Carisbrooke*, carried Bulleid's famous malachite green, and it is generally agreed that the overall effect was pretty frightful!

Martello has had a more restful retirement since leaving Point of Ayr in 1971, for it was one of several of the Butlins engines to go to Bressingham Railway Museum in Norfolk. It was overhauled and returned to working order in time for its centenary in 1975, which was duly celebrated, *Martello* looking very handsome indeed in Marsh umber livery. After several seasons in working order the engine was mothballed and remains a static exhibit in the museum's exhibition shed, still looking very well maintained and in no way disgracing its stablemates.

The late-Brighton style livery, with 'LBSC' on the side tanks, could be faulted; to be rigidly authentic, the only livery *Martello* could carry would have to be the final BR one, as it was not fitted with its ex-Isle of Wight bunker (saved from

Wonersh when it was scrapped) until 1961. However, it is a small point and the effective answer is that *Martello*, the only 'Terrier' currently carrying Marsh livery, shows how very dignified they look in it.

By contrast, *Knowle* has had a nomadic existence, quite out of the public eye, since leaving Minehead. The seemingly obvious home, as it was right on the doorstep, was the West Somerset Railway, then a very new member of the preserved railway industry. *Knowle* duly moved in 1975 and went to Williton for overhaul. Two things soon became obvious, however. One was that *Knowle*, like *Brighton*, had rather suffered during its seaside sojourn. The other was that while the infant WSR was desperate for motive power, a little 0-6-0T would not really do what it needed. With the prospect of a 22-mile line with some long, steep gradients and the need for four-coach trains, *Knowle* was outclassed before it ever ran.

Not surprisingly, the WSR turned its efforts to restoring larger engines and in 1983 began to look round for someone who might want to take the 'Terrier' off its hands. The eventual purchaser was Rick Edmondson, a director of the railway restoration company Resco and owner of a number of other items of stock. *Knowle* moved again, this time to outer London, then making its way to Resco's premises and finally, in the early 1990s, to the Kent & East Sussex. Restoration took place at Rolvenden and *Knowle* returned to service in April 1999, after 26 years in limbo, the longest service break to date of any 'Terrier'.

The KESR is a suitable home for *Knowle* for the engine did a long stint of service on the line. Hired out by the SR in 1940, it was still there at Nationalisation. The indignity of derailing near Wittersham Road and nearly sinking into an adjoining marsh in 1949 ended the stay but once

repaired it was soon back and spent most of the 1950-8 period allocated to KESR duties.

Of 10 surviving 'Terriers', seven are on working railways where they all have parts to play in the operation. While it is highly unlikely that anyone will add to the class by building replicas, it is also improbable that their numbers will decrease in the foreseeable future. The most vulnerable part of a steam engine, the boiler, can be replaced and it is now proved beyond doubt that this can be done with the 'Terriers'. Patterns for new wheels have been made and a pattern for cylinder blocks is being made at the time of writing. The components of a 'Terrier' most likely to wear out and (previously) the most difficult to replace, can now be reproduced. There is no reason why the survivors should not be steaming a long way into the 21st century. If they are not exactly reproducing their original working conditions for future generations of enthusiasts and visitors, then at least they will remain an attractive and lasting testimonial to the quality of Victorian design and engineering, as practised by that master locomotive builder, William Stroudley.

Above:
Once back in service, *Stepney* became a popular member of the Bluebell fleet. It is seen here with steam to spare, heading up the 1 in 75 climb from Holywell to Horsted Keynes in November 1988, in the guise of *Morden* in its 1950s livery, hauling three SR coaches. *Mike Esau*

Above left:
Bluebell 'Terriers' rarely leave the line, due to concern about possible strain to the frames through being loaded onto road vehicles. However, *Fenchurch* did visit the KESR in September 1981 and is seen leaving Wittersham Road. *Brian Stephenson*

Left:
In late LBSC livery, *Martello* rests in the display hall at Bressingham. Moves are afoot to return the engine to working order. *Carrie Thomas*

Right:
Stepney's long period out of service on the Bluebell Railway was ended largely by public donations to an overhaul fund. The painting of a well-known face on the smokebox door encouraged many youngsters to donate their loose change. *Stepney* probably holds the British Steam Record for the largest percentage of an overhaul paid for by children! *Mike Esau*

Above:
With construction work still ongoing, *Waddon* stands alongside one of its new companions, SNCF 0-6-0 No C841, in 1966. *Canadian Railway Museum/ Ian Allan Library*

Below:
Hunslet 'Austerity' No 23 dwarfs *Sutton* as the pair cross Newmill Bridge with a Wittersham Road-Tenterden train in September 1977.
Brian Morrison

Above:
Martello and new stablemate *Duchess of Sutherland* are shunted together at Ayr, pending the move to the holiday camp. *Derek Cross/R. C. Riley Collection*

Below:
On 21 July 1991 *Freshwater* took part in an historic event, the opening of the new Smallbrook Junction station, which marked the extension of the Steam Railway from Haven Street and the establishment of cross-platform connection with the BR Island Line. The 'Terrier' is seen pulling away to run round its train, the first two vehicles of which are restored historic four-wheelers. *Stuart Duddy*

CHAPTER SEVEN

The Story Goes On

The 'Terriers' in preservation; discussed by the people who work with them

BILL BROPHY, Shedmaster, Bluebell Railway

Bill Brophy can claim a longer involvement with preserved 'Terriers' than anyone else, for he accompanied *Stepney* on its journey to the Bluebell Railway.

Bill was an engineering apprentice at Eastleigh Works in 1960 when, early in the year, *Stepney*, which had just been sold to the Bluebell as its first engine, was put through the Works for an overhaul before dispatch to Sheffield Park (shades of Brighton 60 years previously). The shop floor staff were clearly pleased that this surplus engine was to have a further lease of life and entered into the spirit of the event. More, perhaps, was done to *Stepney* than was strictly essential. What was certainly done, and without the knowledge of the Works authorities, was that various useful spares were placed aboard *Stepney* before departure. Perhaps 'smuggled aboard' would be better! Injectors and other small but vital spares were hidden under the coal and suspended from wires in the water tanks.

Then the awful thought occurred — what if the Bluebell people in their innocence wrote to Eastleigh to thank them for their generosity? It was quickly arranged that a couple of the apprentices should accompany *Stepney* on its journey to Sheffield Park, ostensibly to keep an eye on the behaviour of the newly-overhauled engine but mainly to warn the Bluebell people to keep their mouths shut about the 'extras'. Bill and Malcolm Knight were chosen.

Stepney made that historic journey under its own steam in May, making overnight stops at Fratton and Brighton and arriving on the Bluebell with two coaches, the railway's first stock, picked up at Brighton. Once there, Bill was quickly approached by General Manager Horace May and Locomotive Foreman Jack Owen, and asked if he would like to come down to help. Looking around, he realised that the railway, while possessing plenty of enthusiasm, was rather short on engineering experience (this was after all the administrative south of England, not the industrial north), realised that he could be useful, and agreed. Nearly 40 years later, he is still there, his

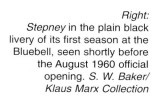

Right:
Stepney in the plain black livery of its first season at the Bluebell, seen shortly before the August 1960 official opening. *S. W. Baker/ Klaus Marx Collection*

involvement with the 'Terriers' having lasted far longer than he could ever have believed in early 1960.

Stepney was Bluebell's only engine at first, he recalls, the infant company hoping that it could get by until it could afford another. However, BR's decision that its new neighbour could not operate into Horsted Keynes, which station was still served by the hourly electric service from Haywards Heath, rather changed matters. With no run-round facility at the north end of its line, the Bluebell was forced to adopt a novel operating practice, an engine at each end of the train, the trailing engine being pulled along as a dead load. This meant an urgent approach to BR for another engine; astonishingly BR decided that it could not spare another 'Terrier' out of the 11 remaining, and offered the line ex-SECR 'P' No 31323 instead. Thus began a friendly rivalry between Brighton and South Eastern camps on the Bluebell Loco Department, in which Bill admits cheerfully that he is on the South Eastern side, mainly because Jack Owen, for many years the Locomotive Foreman, was strongly pro-Brighton! Bill still contends that the 'Ps' are better engines from a footplateman's point of view, though he adds that, of course, they were designed 35 years later, with the benefit of evolution of design.

Above:
Throughout its first period of Bluebell service, *Stepney's* Stroudley livery seemed not quite right. One oddity was the bunker number, painted on in duplicate list style. The engine is seen in Sheffield Park coal dock in 1965, with Locomotive Foreman Jack Owen looking on pensively. *R. C. Riley*

Top:
Due to the vagaries of overhauling steam engines in the post-steam age, *Fenchurch's* centenary celebrations had to be held a couple of months late. On 7 September 1972, the actual centenary day of its entry into traffic, the engine is being worked on in the Bluebell's old repair shed, with a blackboard marking the significance of the date. *Mike Esau*

How would Bill describe the 'Terriers'?

A 'Terrier' is a thinking man's engine, not really one for beginners, he says. Being so small, if something goes amiss, the problem escalates quickly. He realised that himself on that first run along the Sussex Coast; he had some footplate experience by then but to him a small engine was an 'N' class Mogul. Dealing with something about a third of the size started him off on a sharp learning curve.

Having to crouch on the floor to get a proper look at what the fire was doing was a novel experience, especially in that small cab, where he quickly learned where the hot pipes were! 'The firebox is not very forgiving. It is shallow and relatively long, and with that low door it is tricky to see if you have an even fire. The common mistake is to let a ridge form half way down the box, then no coal gets to the front and the front burns thin. Before you know it, you've got a hole in the front of the fire and cold air rushing through the tubes, and your pressure's falling away fast. It's also a good way to get leaking tube

ends.' The art, he says, is to fire evenly in small amounts and keep an eye on the chimney top; a light grey smoke is ideal — once the exhaust goes clear you know you've got problems. 'Lots of firemen have had to resort to the fire-irons to spread the fire over the grate and build up again. But it's a bad habit, it breaks up the fire and forms too much clinker. A "Terrier's" firebars are close together and likely to clinker up anyway. One trick is to put in a shovel or so of ballast before lighting the fire. The stone shatters in the heat and forms a layer between the bars and the fire

which catches the clinker and stops the bars burning.' They are, he adds, reasonably easy to fire on the move, 'but only if you're a small or medium fireman'.

The injectors give problems too. Not designed or originally fitted, they are rather large for the boiler. Not only will they fill it quickly, with a risk of priming, but they will knock back the boiler pressure — you can actually watch the needle go back — so you need to know the right places to use them. 'The controls are not user-friendly,' he adds. 'The overflow pipe is under the front of the water tank, so you can only see it by leaning out and looking ahead. The water control is not a wheel but a lever with a locking wing-nut, so you need two hands to set it. You're setting the water inside the cab while leaning out to see if you've got it right and you've no hands left to hold on with — it's not a comfortable working position.'

Water has been a critical factor from the start, he recalls. 'In the first season we had to water the engines from a hosepipe on the platforms and the timetable was based on how long it took to fill the tanks. Now, with a regular supply of water only at Sheffield Park, the 18 miles to Kingscote and back is approaching the limit of a "Terrier". It really limits them to two-coach trains now, or they use too much water.' In the past *Fenchurch* would take three coaches to Horsted Keynes, and even four on rare special occasions.

Bunker capacity can be a similar problem. 'At first it was a matter of pride to work a day without going back on shed for more coal, though this was helped by *Stepney's* coal rails. We would build up the bunker top with a wall of large pieces of coal, piling up inside this and even heaping it up on the cab floor, and you should be able to run for a day. Then of course all coaling was done by hand, with baskets. Now we use fork lift trucks and it is far quicker but you cannot get through the day on one load and the timetable does not really give time to go back on shed to fill up with coal.'

On the driver's side of the footplate, the regulator poses a challenge. 'They can be very stiff to move, a real two-hand job, *Stepney's* is a real pain. The only answer is to wriggle it gently open or else you get too much at once and the engine primes.' The lever reverser gives problems too. Nobody wants to run an engine in full gear all the time and notching up a 'Terrier' is not easy. 'The engine will try to pull the lever into full gear

Above:
The fireman hands over the single line staff, as *Fenchurch* drifts into Horsted Keynes in the evening of 20 November 1983. The bulk of the LNWR observation car behind the 'Terrier' is reminiscent of a Brighton motor train balloon coach. *Mike Esau*

Right:
Much of the Bluebell's traffic is now beyond the 'Terriers' but plenty of work is still found for them. *Fenchurch* is seen engaged in a day's shunting at Horsted Keynes in 1982. *Mike Esau*

Left:
A mid-1980s view of *Fenchurch* piloting *Stepney* through the woods on the way to Horsted Keynes. *Mike Esau*

Right:
Two classics of Victorian locomotive design work together, as *Stepney* pilots LSWR Adams radial tank No 488 on the approaches to Horsted Keynes in September 1985. The irony is that No 488 was one of the radial tanks to work successfully on the Lyme Regis branch, where the 'Terriers' had been found wanting, partly because of their longer fixed wheelbase.
Mike Esau

Right:
Fenchurch is seen at Sheffield Park in July 1994, being dismantled for the overhaul which is currently in hand.
Mike Esau

Below:
The 'Terrier'/'P' comparison can be made at the KESR as well as the Bluebell. *Sutton* and No 1556 round Willow Curve, double-heading a Tenterden-Wittersham Road train in May 1988. *Brian Stephenson*

if steam is on. The easy way is to shut off steam and move the lever, then open up again but other loco staff might spot you if you do that; if you shut off steam on a "Terrier", it squeaks at the chimney. It's a matter of pride to be able to notch up with steam on. There's a place to rest your foot and you have to grab the lever and snatch it between exhaust beats. If you miss, it will drag you forward, hard. It's not for the faint-hearted.'

'Terriers' developed various braking permutations during their long careers and the Bluebell's pair show this. *Stepney* is vacuum fitted only, *Fenchurch* has air and vacuum brakes. The vacuum brake has an interesting trick, warns Bill. 'It was not an original fitting, so the exhaust steam pipe from the vacuum ejector runs along the outside of the boiler. When the ejector is off, steam left in the pipe soon cools and condenses. If you put the ejector on sharply, this water is blown out in a rush, picks up soot in the smokebox and gives anyone standing near a black shower-bath. It's not good public relations — tends to cause Irate Passenger Syndrome! You need to put the blower on first, then ease the ejector open, to disperse any water in the pipe.

'The air brake is a good brake but you have to remember that it is only going to work as long as there is air pressure in the auxiliary reservoir. You can apply it in stages but if you release it, it all goes, and if you want to cut back the brake force, you have to drop the brake and then build up again. This uses your air and unless you put the lever right back so the triple valve throws over and recharges the reservoir, you can suddenly have no brake. This has caught drivers out in the past, which explains some of the buffer-strikes at terminus stations.

'*Fenchurch's* Westinghouse air pump has a trick, which is to squirt splashes of oil onto the top cab step. If you forget about this, you might be reminded when you sit down rather suddenly. The pump can stick sometimes and needs a thump to start it.' (That is why the pump top has a few dents!) 'It brings back memories of Stewart's Lane, where some engines had their pumps mounted further forward and mostly had big dents where the crews had shied something like a lump of coal to get a sticking pump to start. Yet French steam engines had their air pumps totally enclosed, and they never gave trouble — I wonder what their secret was.'

As Shedmaster, Bill has no qualms about rostering a 'Terrier' for a duty within its abilities. 'They're reliable because they are such basic engines — far less to go wrong. You cannot think of them as a class of two, they are individual machines. *Fenchurch* with its larger cylinders is the more powerful but it means that it uses more water, so that can limit what you ask it to do. If you work them too hard in the summer there is a fire risk from thrown cinders while in winter the steam heat puts an extra demand for water, so the two-coach limit is really a sensible one. Anyway, they are such historic machines that it would be wrong to over-stretch them on a regular basis.

'The longer run [to Kingscote] has not caused any mechanical problems. It means that the fireman has to be more alert though. For one thing the gradient changes from a climb to a fall at the north end of Sharpthorne Tunnel. If you are not going to risk a dry firebox crown as the engine starts downhill and the driver shuts off, you must put the injectors on about half-way through the tunnel.'

Mechanically, the pair show up individual oddities. *Stepney's* exhaust, through its replica Stroudley chimney, sounds different from either cylinder, giving a sort of 'phee, phoo, phee, phoo'

effect. 'Nobody knows why,' says Bill. *Fenchurch*, with a Marsh-style cast-iron chimney, makes a different noise altogether. *Fenchurch* brought a particular problem with it into preservation, in the form of its original wrought-iron wheel centres. When a crack was found at the end of its last period of service, this caused a major problem. Finding an expert who could repair a wrought-iron wheel centre proved impossible and it cannot be welded. The only option was to make a pattern and cast new steel wheel centres, as was done to others in late Brighton and SR days. 'The crack might have been there for decades and could perhaps have stayed trouble-free for decades more, but once we knew about it we had to put it right.'

Another looming problem is in the cylinders; both blocks are getting thin on top, after years of being attacked at the bottom of the smokebox. 'The layer of concrete at the bottom of the box does not stop the rusting and can trap acid damp. A new pattern for 'Terrier' cylinders is being made but it takes time and *Fenchurch's* old block may have to go back for the time being. It

Below:
When *Newport* first returned to the Isle of Wight from Butlins, it went to Ryde Works for a planned cosmetic overhaul, as Haven Street then had virtually no facilities. It is seen in the Works on 10 March 1973. *Roger Silsbury*

Above:
Double-headed 'Terriers' run into Haven Street from Wootton in August 1989, both engines carrying appropriate pre-Grouping livery. The IoW Steam Railway continues the later island tradition of all engines running chimney first from Ryde Pier Head.
Stuart Duddy

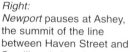

Right:
Newport pauses at Ashey, the summit of the line between Haven Street and Smallbrook Junction, with a train for Smallbrook in August 1993. *Stuart Duddy*

is thin but it has not yet got to the state of the last 'T9s', which are said to have ended their days with the top of the bores being polished concrete!'

In all, Bill feels, the Bluebell's 'Terriers' have been a good investment. '*Stepney's* publicity value alone is enormous.' Inevitably, he makes a comparison with the 'P' class, while stressing that the latter is a more modern design so you should expect improvements. He does not agree with the common claim that the 'P' design was based on the 'Terriers'. There are, he says, only a certain number of shapes available in designing a small 0-6-0 tank! 'The "P" is an easier engine all round; the deeper firebox is easier to fire and more forgiving of mistakes; the injectors are better, the engine rides better and there is more room in the cab. The balance of critical dimensions — boiler output, cylinder size and adhesion, is about right, as it is in the "Terriers", though *Fenchurch* shows at times that the bigger cylinders throw things out of balance. And the steam reverser on a "P" is a great help too, especially appreciated when you are shunting.'

LEN PULLINGER, Chief Engineer, Isle of Wight Steam Railway

Len has also had a long association with preserved 'Terriers', as he has worked full-time on the IoW Steam Railway since its earliest days — he was, in fact, the infant company's first employee.

Len pre-dates the railway's 'Terriers' and remembers them both arriving — in very different states — and saw through their returns to service, since when he has worked steadily to improve their performance and behaviour, back to what he believes Stroudley intended. Len has a more demanding task than his opposite numbers at the Bluebell and Kent & East Sussex. While the Bluebell has evolved into a 'large engine' railway and the KESR has a reasonable sized fleet in which the 'Terriers' are at the small end, the IoW is very much a victim of history. Its loco fleet is small in both senses; at the time of writing it depended on just three ex-main line engines, the two 'Terriers' and the sole surviving 'O2' *Calbourne*, with a Hunslet 'Austerity' 0-6-0ST providing top-end power and a couple of smaller industrials in the wings. Not surprisingly, the line concentrates on keeping time out of traffic as short as possible, although this is usually affected by factors outside the workshop's control.

Here is still a line where a 'Terrier' is capable of working the service for much of the year, so as such they remain front-line motive power.

Perhaps as a result they get more intense works attention than their sisters elsewhere. Since the early 1980s, Len and his team have had more need and opportunity to study the art of getting a 'Terrier' to give of its best, which, he says, you do by making sure that all the components which affect performance are absolutely right. A properly set-up 'Terrier', says Len, is twice as good as one which has gone off a bit.

Both, of course, are ex-island 'Terriers', No 11 (*Newport*) being *Brighton*, one of the most historic members of the class, and No 8 (*Freshwater*) being the much-travelled *Newington*. It seems right to use their current identities here.

No 11 arrived first, in early 1973, but was not to return to service until 1989. The ex-Pwllheli Butlins 'Terrier', it was designated for the IoW as the most appropriate home; a cosmetic restoration was the first plan but once a return to service was decided on, the engine was purchased outright from Butlins and a full restoration commenced. Len is particularly grateful that there were still a few of the old

Below:
An almost perfect re-creation of the late 1930s as *Freshwater* climbs away from Haven Street for Wootton in August 1994. *Stuart Duddy*

Newport Works staff, who had worked on the 'Terriers' in the old days, alive and active when work began, and that they willingly weighed in and passed on their experience.

No 11 had suffered badly from the habit of young boys (mainly) at Butlins of seeing if they could lob stones into the chimney. Too many of them succeeded! Some of the stones fell down the blastpipe and dropped through the ports into the cylinders. When No 11 was moved as the first stage of its journey back south, these stones jammed the bore, breaking off an entire corner of the cylinder block, wrecking the piston and bending the piston rod. Nine years standing in the open near the sea caused other problems as well.

No 8, following its sojourn as a pub sign, arrived in mid-1979 and Len remembers clearly the evidence of its last steaming in 1966: not only was the boiler full of water but the cinders remained in the grate and the ash in the ashpan! That well-boiled water may in fact have done much to preserve the boiler and firebox in good order, and Len found that the engine was in pretty fair mechanical order, far better than No 11. Attention was turned to No 8; she was steamed the following year and re-entered service in 1981.

Since return to service, No 8 has missed only four seasons (including reboilering in 1997) and No 11 just one; a tribute to the engines and the Works — but Len agrees that it has been hard work at times!

Len has his own view on why the 'Terriers' have had such long lives. 'It's the wrought-iron frames,' he says. 'The metal is more resilient than steel, particularly old steels, and has been able to take more punishment than such light frames would have taken if they had been steel. The axleboxes and horns are the old type without adjustable wedges to take up wear, so as wear occurs the boxes start to batter against the frames. Steel frames would be likely to crack at the horn corners under these conditions but the wrought-iron ones stood up to it.' So the engines did not go the way of many other classes that had been reduced to secondary duties, being withdrawn as not worth repairing when their frames developed cracks. He does not think that the needs of the Hayling Island line would have saved them. 'If they had started to suffer cracked frames, then something would have been found to take their place, or Langstone Bridge would have been upgraded to take something a little heavier.'

The wrought-iron wheel centres cause him slightly more concern. 'There are cracks in them

but that is the nature of the metal. The wheels have been examined, the cracks are all recorded and monitored, and they're not getting any worse. Some of them have probably been there since the wheels were forged. If any of them start to get worse, we'll have to make a decision. Thanks to Bluebell there is now a pattern for casting new centres, so we will have that as an option, which we did not before.'

With the long term in mind, Len welcomes the making of a new cylinder block pattern. 'Our cylinder blocks are pretty good but they have corroded on top and won't last for ever. We have a hand in the project to make a new pattern, it's all part of ensuring that the engines have a long-term future.'

Len has a high regard for Stroudley's original design. 'The "Terrier" design includes some clever ideas. One is the positioning of the steam ports. They are not symmetrical to the centre point of slide valve travel but slightly offset, to compensate for the volume taken up at one end by the piston rod. Making the back port slightly longer gives an equal pull from front and back. You notice it particularly when notched up; the effort and exhaust are more even than in some other small designs.

'Another good design feature is the motion plate. It is not at the back end of the slide bars but towards their centre. This not only gives the bars better support where the main thrust is, it also allows the valve gear to have longer motion rods — and the longer the distance between eccentrics and link, the better the valve events you can get, with less distortion. In a small engine like a "Terrier" this has made a big difference.'

Early experience with No 8 (which was none too keen on work when first restored) taught the Works team the importance of getting things just right on a 'Terrier'. 'It had problems at the front end. The blastpipe, slide valves, piston rings, all had to be worked on to get them right — alignment, positioning and so on — but when all was set up it was a different engine. You soon know if one item is going wrong — you go out on a train, and oh, dear!'

Sloppy valve gear, with worn faces and pins, can cause serious problems too, says Len. It should be possible to run a 'Terrier' notched up almost to mid gear, but it cannot be done if there is slop in the motion. 'You can lose up to half the port opening, and apart from sounding and feeling terrible, it just won't pull.'

Getting the valve gear properly set up is just as important. 'All the manuals seem to base valve setting on Walschaerts gear and it is as if the first principles of setting Stephenson Link were forgotten when Walschaerts and other radial gears became common. So we left the book on the shelf and taught ourselves link valve gear setting from scratch. It's made a big difference. We can run them notched right up and we get a nice quiet exhaust, which is what they should have; the idea that they have barking exhaust beats and that's why they were called "Terriers" is quite wrong.'

No 8 received a new boiler in 1998, one of two built for 'Terriers' by Israel Newton (the other being for the KESR's *Bodiam*). Closely following the *Marsh* boiler design, it is, says Len, better than expected. 'It is a super steam raiser. It has four fewer tubes than the old one and the inner firebox is different. It is steel, not copper, has a flat top rather than the sloping Marsh top, and there is more room for steam release in the water legs round the box. The tubes were sacrificed to get a better radius on the corners and it has all worked out very well, at least as free-steaming as the old one.' There was some concern that modern boiler insurance regulations would kick at Salter safety valves being fitted to a new boiler and Len was prepared to have Drummond-style 'lock-up' valves, which would have returned No 8 to its appearance in FYNR and early SR days. However, as the KESR wanted Salter valves, Newton's designed them in and the insurers approved without a problem. 'The only difficulty was the dome flange,' says Len. 'The insurers insisted that this was to BS5931, which made it a bigger diameter than the original. We just managed to get it to fit under the dome cover!'

No 8's old boiler and *Bodiam's* are now both at Haven Street and Len plans to use the best parts of both to make a spare boiler, in reserve for No 11. 'No 11's is a rather odd boiler. It has patches in the firebox, fitted in BR days, we are not sure exactly why, and they make it a bit of an unknown quantity. It is closely watched but we cannot be sure how long it will last, so it will be a great help to have another boiler ready to take its place.'

The boilers are not particularly easy for regular maintenance. 'We wash out our boilers every 10 working days, more often than most lines but we have very hard water. We like to inspect the fireboxes at the same time, especially No 11's, and to get in you have to unbolt the firedoor from the backhead. The Marsh boilers are not particularly easy to wash out; the top plugs are badly placed.'

A few other features, mainly BR modifications, do not find favour at Haven Street. 'They are fitted with big Ashford-type steam valves, which are not so well sited or so easy to maintain as the ones they carried in SR days. The clack valves are a double-clack design, again not original, and they need lapping in at every 1,000-mile exam to keep them working properly. The injectors themselves are far too big and can be a problem for the inexperienced. The water valves are good but they're in the way if you need to get inside the tank!'

The IoW is an air brake line and Len has had few problems with the air pumps, though the 'Terriers' carry a small size which can be more mischievous than the larger ones. They are also still fitted with the original style driver's brake valves, which are easier to use than the later Westinghouse types and give a better control of train pipe pressure.

In overall workshop terms, Len finds the 'Terriers' take more time than the 'O2' but much less than the industrials. On the road, they can prove awkward for inexperienced crews, 'but once you have mastered them, you will have an easier day than on anything else. Yes, as they are small engines, things will happen fast if they play up, but they are able to do a big engine's job in a small package. They are masters of the traffic for most of the time and their economy is excellent — they will do a day's work on less than a ton of coal including lighting up, unless you overload them. You set them the work for which they were intended, or you pay the price in a soaring coal bill. If a third one became available, yes, I'd definitely welcome it.' Both the pair have the larger 14in cylinders fitted to many of the class and Len says that the extra power is an important part of their success on the IoW.

The 'Terriers' have been part of the island scene long enough for legends to grow and Len remembers two late enthusiasts of the IoW lines, A. B. MacLeod and Sir Peter Allen. The pair had a lively argument about No 11's livery when it was cosmetically restored in the 1970s, carrying IWC black with the lettering shaded green. Both could remember the IWC; one said the shading was correct, the other insisted it should be brown. The argument raged on. In despair, Len turned to a retired island railwayman, who had commenced his career on the IWC. Was the green shading correct? 'Yes, that's right,' he said. 'Or it could be brown — that would be right too.' At least it stopped the argument!

LEWIS NODES, Locomotive Dept, Bluebell Railway

A member of the Bluebell Railway Locomotive Department, Lewis heads a team of volunteers who have now overhauled or restored several of the line's smaller engines. Belonging to the last generation who can remember much of BR steam, Lewis has been an active volunteer since the 1970s. His gang began serious work on *Fenchurch* after the return to service of the SECR 'C' class, their previous project, in 1994.

Fenchurch has had some surprises for them, says Lewis, with evidence of its past which cannot be explained, especially since so many of the class's drawings have vanished over the years. For instance, the cylinder block is a 14in Billinton one fitted in 1904; so they were surprised to find evidence of a condenser take-off union on the block top. Billinton removed the condensers when 'Terriers' went through the Works, so why did his cylinder blocks have this fitting? It seems that everyone who might know is now dead. Another surprise was that some motion parts still showed signs of the old feedwater pump fittings. The pumps were removed early in the century, so why were parts fitted later that would accommodate them? Surely it was not all down to using up old stock?

Fenchurch's restoration is in the hands of volunteers mainly because it would have to wait years for a place in the main workshop programme and yet it is a popular engine, especially with many of the Loco Department. The crucial event was the successful appeal for money to have the new wheel centre pattern made, done in memory of Matthew 'Chip' Wood, a young member of the department who died suddenly; *Fenchurch* was his favourite

engine. The new wheels are now fitted to the axles and stand waiting to go back under the frames. Their paint gives away one of Lewis's plans: *Fenchurch* will be turned out in Marsh umber livery.

More than that, it will be turned out in the guise of a Marsh-era 'A1'. The key to this is that the smokebox needs replacing. 'They don't last all that long,' explains Lewis. So the opportunity is being taken to make and fit a Stroudley-style smokebox, with wingplates, raised sandboxes and all. Effectively, *Fenchurch* will be like *Waddon*, an 'A1' with an 'A1X' boiler. It is a new guise for *Fenchurch*, which has never carried Marsh livery before. 'It opens other opportunities,' says Lewis, 'such as Stroudley yellow or even goods green, in the future.' It will have dummy condenser pipes, as reinstated by Marsh, fitted. What about the chimney? 'We would like a Stroudley copper-top if we can get one made that is correct. There's a lot of work goes into one, mainly shaping the copper. We have said that the conversion will not add to the cost of the restoration so we were going to use the cast-iron chimney again but we have had enough in donations to afford the new chimney.'

The old cylinder block is being used again but, says Lewis, this will be its last time. 'The problem is the steam pipe union, which has badly corroded away. It has been repaired before — three times, we think. Another repair has been managed but now there is simply no metal left to do it again.'

The new cylinder block will interest historians, for the pattern is for the original Stroudley 13in bore, unlike the current 14in or *Stepney's* Marsh 12in block. It will give a new chance to assess original 'Terrier' performance. 'Shunting will be the test. *Stepney* is not a good shunting engine; it hasn't got the initial punch.'

Fenchurch should enter service in its new guise in 2000, probably between Easter and June. No doubt its changed appearance will lead to some lively debate but it will certainly add some variety to the 'Terrier' scene.

RICK EDMONDSON, owner of *Knowle*

An engineer by profession, Rick Edmondson has been involved in various aspects of railway work for years. He is perhaps best known to enthusiasts as one of the founders of Resco, the company he still operates, which began as providing engineering services to the preservation movement as well as other branches of the railway industry, and is now much involved in the testing and certification of locomotives and stock for Railtrack.

Rick is also unique as the only individual to own a 'Terrier'; the other nine all being owned by societies, companies or corporate bodies. It is sometimes forgotten that he also owns a major share in a somewhat larger engine, the famous BR Pacific *Britannia*. Like *Knowle*, it was bought at a time when its future was problematical and Resco was looking for an engineering challenge.

To the question, why has he become the owner of *Knowle*, Rick explains that it was all to do with the development of Resco. The company was first set up by him and Mike Hart (now of Railway Wheelsets in Rotherham) and business in the early days in the late 1970s was mainly at the industrial shunting engine end of the market. With the directors having an interest in preservation, they wanted to expand into contract work for preserved lines and decided to prove themselves with demonstration projects. First tackled was the restoration of a District Railway four-wheel carriage, then the Manning Wardle 0-6-0ST *Charwelton*, both of which are now part of the regular active fleet at the Kent & East Sussex. They then looked round for something more ambitious.

This was the time, in the early 1980s, when a group on the West Somerset had begun the restoration of *Knowle* but as things progressed it became apparent that the task was much more demanding than it had appeared and that the loco would be of little use to the WSR anyway. Discouraged, they put it up for sale. Rick

Edmondson was the eventual buyer and the dismantled 'Terrier' left Somerset for Resco's Southeast London workshops.

Being largely dismantled, the first job, Rick recalls, was to 'spread it out on the floor and see what was there!' Once the bits were counted and the odd missing part noted, the project began. The method was to overhaul, mend or restore all parts, fittings and components before thinking of reassembly; 'that's the best way of tackling a restoration like this,' says Rick.

The platework was in an appalling state — the result of those years of bracing sea breezes at Minehead — and needed almost total replacement. The cab roof was one of the few pieces that could be saved. A new bunker was made which would have been unique on a 'Terrier'; about half-way between the original and the Isle of Wight one fitted in later years. The boiler was in a poor state, particularly around the front tubeplate, and went to an outside contractor for a rebuild; 'I won't say which one, because they did a poor job. When the boiler was tested at the KESR it was obviously not fit for use and giving it another repair is one of the things that has delayed *Knowle's* return to service.'

With many parts refurbished, initial reassembly did not seem too far away when Resco took a different turn. The opportunity was taken to expand and buy another company. Consolidating took up all the available time and preservation work was set aside for a while. Shortly after this, *Britannia* was bought, as one of those once-only and unmissable opportunities. With starting to sort that out, plus the contract to construct the replica *Iron Duke* for the National Railway Museum, preservation priorities had to be re-assessed. *Knowle's* bits went back into a container.

Events took another turn when Resco sought to buy the closed Gravesend West branch with a view to operating a tourist service. *Knowle* would have been ideal for this operation but sadly the project fell through, partly due to difficulties in making working agreements with BR. This left the company with around three miles of good track including points and crossings, just at the time that the Kent & East Sussex was looking for rail for its extension to Northiam. Rick has had a long affection for the KESR. Indeed, the line first fired his interest in railways, and preservation in particular, when as a young man he discovered one of its ungated level crossings and began exploring to see what it was all about. He was soon volunteering and was to become a director of the company for some years, before expanding business interests ate up his free time. He was happy to sell the redundant track to the KESR and discussions then moved on to *Knowle* and the possibility of a home for the loco on the KESR.

An agreement was reached, that *Knowle* would move to the railway (perhaps 'move back' would be a better way of putting it) and that the Works at Rolvenden would complete its rebuild, doing the work as a contract job for Rick. It was also agreed that it would be a 'filler' job, that is, there was no set completion date and the railway staff would be free to press on with it when time allowed, or leave it when the demands of the operating fleet needed their attention. So *Knowle*, which moved to Rolvenden at the start of the 1990s, only entered service in 1999.

The work was done in close consultation with Rick. 'We have taken a realistic approach,' he says. 'Mechanically we have not aimed to put the engine back to its condition on such-and-such a date, this is the latest of its many overhauls. Changes have been made in the light of developments over the years and we have added a few more to these. But the engine is still *Knowle*.'

Changes have included fixing a few defects which have caused wear over the years. Also some brasswork and nonferrous fittings have gone missing, probably stolen, at some time since the engine last worked. Appropriate replacements have been fitted, rather than replicas being made. The steam valves on the boiler top are examples. 'We aim to have the engine better than new; we have kept up the railway works tradition of making alterations to keep the engine in service. *Knowle* is not a museum piece and will be entering service to do a real job.'

Knowle remains dual-braked, with both Westinghouse air pump and Dreadnought ejector.

The intermediate-size bunker has been replaced with an original Stroudley type. The engine was due, at the time of writing, to re-enter service at Easter 1999. At present it retains the Drummond chimney but planned livery changes in the future will almost impel a replica original 'copper-top' to be made.

The engine was turned out in SR Bulleid black livery in response to a special request but different liveries will be carried. Rick wants to see *Knowle* in full Stroudley livery before long, complete with its name and original No 78. It is being main-line registered through Resco, although Rick regrets that it is not very likely to do any serious main line running — 'and certainly not at the 50mph-plus speeds of the past!'

The KESR, says Rick, will remain the engine's home but he hopes that it will make visits to other lines. One of his great dreams is to arrange a major event with all the surviving 'Terriers' brought together, possibly even *Waddon*, which he feels is no longer getting the appreciation it deserves in Canada. 'Its possible repatriation should be investigated,' he declares.

Like a growing number of 'Terrier' admirers, Rick never saw the class at work on BR, first encountering them in preservation. He has grown to have a great respect for them and says that they are among the most elegant of British designs. After the uncertainties of its early preserved career, *Knowle* has ended up in good hands.

Below:
Double-headed 'Terriers' on the KESR: *Bodiam* leads *Sutton* past the crayfish farm on the approaches to Rolvenden. A third member of the class, *Knowle*, will soon allow more permutations of such scenes as this. *Mike Esau*

Above and left:
Two views of *Fenchurch's* frames during the current overhaul at Sheffield Park. The relative lightness of the engine's foundations is evident, especially with the large slots cut between the axleboxes to reduce weight. With the cylinder block removed for repair, the motion plate can be seen between the frames. *Author*

Right:
Still in Stroudley condition, *Bookham* is seen at Littlehampton in 1894. *LGRP/Bucknall Collection*

CHAPTER EIGHT

'Terriers' Assessed

Of all the hundreds of pre-Grouping locomotive classes, only a tiny minority have survived, whether active or in museums. The Brighton, with examples of four classes (and plans for a replica of another) has done better than most. The 'Terriers' though, are the outstanding example. No other pre-grouping class, let alone a mid-Victorian one, approaches its record of 10 survivors.

The class is now more than 125 years old and the key word to its survival is 'versatility'. Stroudley got the original design almost exactly right and after the loss of their original work they proved equally good, and very economical, in other spheres.

The class as built had just one major weakness, which it shared with other Stroudley classes: the inability to fill its boiler while stationary. Contemporaries of Stroudley who also avoided injectors mostly fitted steam-driven donkey pumps of some description; 'Terriers' had to depend on the pumps driven by the motion, which could lead to the spectacle of an engine scuttling up and down the release roads at Victoria or London Bridge to bring up the water level in the boiler.[1]

[1]This weakness was commented on by the judges of the Paris Exhibition when 'Gladstone' Edward Blount won its gold medal; it is said to be the only thing which prevented it from winning the Supreme Award. Stroudley's riposte was robust: His engines were not designed to remain stationary!

Pumps apart, the 'Terriers' were an example of good design borne out in practice. Small and light, they were powerful for their size as well as being economical to run and to repair. They were robust and their free-running qualities and surprisingly high speed ability made for flexibility in the duties they could perform. The bright livery and aesthetic appeal added to their popularity.

The Stroudley livery was clearly a contentious issue in several quarters. Webb stirred things up when Stroudley presented a paper to the Institution of Civil Engineers, stating that an elaborate livery was a waste of money. Stroudley was well able to deal with that, with figures showing that the cost of the 'decorations' came to less than £1 per locomotive. One feels from this and other recorded exchanges that these two close contemporaries had quite a respect for each other but Webb had perhaps a small axe to grind on the subject of liveries. Ordered by the LNWR directors, while quite new in his post, to abandon the green livery of the Ramsbottom era in favour of black (apparently they thought this would save money), Webb turned a potentially mundane colour scheme into a work of art that was to survive little altered to the end of British steam in 1968 — and was carried by the 'Terriers' in the 1950s. Stroudley by contrast, won the Brighton directors over to his florid livery and not until 16 years after his death did the penny-pinchers on the board, backed by rapidly rising costs and a change in popular tastes, win the day and get the

simpler, more severe, umber livery proposed by Earle Marsh, approved by the directors.

By then of course the 'Terriers' were well into their second phase of service. Some half of the class had outlasted the projected 25-year lifespan and were working the light push-pull motor trains that the LBSC had introduced to compete against road traffic. The measure of the success with which the 'Terriers' and their mini-trains hit back is that for the second time in their careers they outclassed themselves — their services became so popular that larger engines were needed to cope with the demand.

But for these push-pull trains, the LBSC would have withdrawn most of its 'Terriers' by the mid-1900s and this would have been fatal for the class. The few survivors, retained for a limited number of services, would have been vulnerable.

At the Grouping, the 'Terriers' re-entering the fold would not have been additions to a fairly numerous class but a collection of oddities to be replaced as soon as possible. Under those circumstances it is doubtful whether the class would have survived into the 1930s.

One of the puzzles of 'Terrier' history is the time that it took for their second-hand value to be appreciated by the LBSC. Despite the evident success of *Fenchurch* at Newhaven Harbour and *Blackwall* on the Isle of Wight Central, it was several years before redundant 'Terriers' were touted hard on the second-hand market. Sixty years later BR, with perhaps more excuse, was to make the same mistake when it failed at first to spot the resale potential of the class and broke up several of the last survivors.

While it was understandable that impoverished

Above:
One of the classic images of the 'Terriers' must surely be the crossing of Langstone Bridge on the Hayling Island branch. *Mike Esau*

Right:
Dismantled remains of withdrawn engines were a feature of Col Stephens lines in their later years. Here the boilers of *Dido* and *Hecate* are balanced precariously on piles of sleepers, with other bits of the pair scattered about, at Kinnerley, on the Shropshire & Montgomeryshire Railway, in June 1932. *S. W. Baker/ Klaus Marx Collection*

minor railways and even contractors would be tempted by used 'Terriers', the Brighton must have been really surprised to have bids for 30-year-old engines from its moderately friendly neighbour the London & South Western, and from its long-term foe the South Eastern. But Drummond probably reckoned that buying a known quantity was more economical than the drawing office and workshop costs of building two new small engines from scratch, especially with the upheaval of moving the main works from Nine Elms to Eastleigh not yet settled. Similar thinking probably influenced Wainwright at Ashford when he needed a capable little engine for the Sheppey branch. He was sufficiently impressed to design an updated version, the 'P' class 0-6-0Ts, which performed similar work for over 50 years from 1909 to the early 1960s.

Although they never achieved the high profile of the 'Terriers', the eight 'Ps' gave quite a good account of themselves and were to rub shoulders with their more famous counterparts on quite a few occasions after 1923. This continues with the four survivors, preserved at the Bluebell and Kent & East Sussex Railways, where opinions are divided within the Locomotive Departments as to which are the better engines — which suggests (the author is making an effort to be unbiased!) that there is not much in it. Or putting it another way, 35 years after the 'Terriers' appeared, Wainwright was unable to come up with a much better design of the same general size.

By the 1900s another important factor was ensuring the survival of 'Terriers'. They could operate lightly-built and tightly-curved lines in docks, workshop yards and such places where

Left:
An elevated view of *Knowle*, with the later BR 'ferret & dartboard' motif, gives a good study of an 'A1X's' tank-top arrangements.
R. C. Riley

Left:
Finding useful employment as station pilot, *Stepney* is seen in the unusual two-sided platform road at Horsted Keynes while shunting on 27 April 1986.
Brian Morrison

Left:
Fenchurch in the rain at Shildon, 1975. Then basking in the title of the oldest standard gauge engine still in service in Britain, it is close to the then cutting-edge of BR technology, the Advanced Passenger Train, which ironically vanished into ignominious oblivion after huge cost, without ever entering full service.
Mike Esau

Above:
Two 'Terriers' work the LCGB 'South Eastern Ltd' up Tenterden Bank on the KESR on 11 June 1961. *Martello* and *Bodiam* are in charge of a seven-coach train, very much at the limit for a pair of 'Terriers' on the line, especially on that long 1 in 50 climb.
Mike Esau

larger engines were banned. Financial constraints meant that these lines often could not be upgraded and modernised; built cheaply some decades before, they were trapped in what might be called a fiscal time-warp. Once again, why should modern engines be built to do the job when they could be no bigger, and would probably be no better, than the 'Terriers'?

So through the afternoon of the class, it carved out a number of niches for itself. Ironically, the class was to survive beyond its 50th birthday because it was relatively numerous and therefore economic to retain. The main works needed to carry far fewer spares for a class of some 20 engines than for 20 assorted machines and it was practicable to keep a couple of spare boilers on hand, ready overhauled to allow a quick swap and speedy return to service. If a 'Terrier' had to be stopped for attention, another could easily be found and despatched to take its place, in the knowledge that crews and depot staff would be familiar with it. This all helped to reduce operating and maintenance costs, so the 'Terriers' survived.

In fact, more of the engines survived than there

were duties to cover, which explains the long periods in store that some of the class endured in SR days. But anyway, it was a typical feature of the steam age that a class which existed for specific duties would include spare engines.

Works, shed, shunting and docks duties aside, two locations kept the class alive during the SR years and, being passenger operations, also kept them in the public eye. The economic realities of running lines which were unlikely to make much profit ever again, ensured that the investment to replace the 'Terriers' with something more modern was unlikely to be made.

It was further changes to the status quo, rather than the extreme age of the engines, which led to the further decline and final demise of the class in BR days. Traffic patterns changed on the Isle of Wight. Diesel technology had finally reached the point where small and reliable shunting engines could be built and these were to oust the 'Terriers' from pilot duties and the odd dock and industrial siding jobs. A 'Terrier' standing idle for much of the day might not use much coal but a diesel could be switched off and was then even more economical. In the event, it did not matter much, for the lines concerned were soon to close anyway; some even went before the diesels arrived. One by one the traditional haunts of the 'Terriers' were vanishing and this time there would be no new duties to replace them. By the 1960s Hayling Island was the last outpost. It was the complications and expense of retaining

Left:
Sutton and 'P' No 1556 display the Isle of Wight and mainland versions of 1930s SR livery as applied to the company's smallest passenger tank classes, as they head down Tenterden Bank, KESR, on 7 May 1988.
Brian Stephenson

Above:
Last minute attention for *Fenchurch* before it pilots *Stepney* from Sheffield Park, Bluebell Railway.
Mike Esau

vintage steam operation for this branch or the heavy capital cost of upgrading it to take modern traction that led to its closure in November 1963 and the withdrawal of the last 'Terriers'.

Rebuilds to the class over the years made relatively minor changes to appearance, the biggest of all being the new boiler and smokebox designed by Marsh. After Marsh's departure hardly any innovations were made but this had more to do with the class's low status in the overall scheme of things than an arrival at perfection! Maunsell, Bulleid and Riddles all had more important things on their minds than the further development of a class of elderly tank engines that pottered around odd corners of the system. Thus the only other significant change to the 'Terriers' was the enlarged bunkers devised and fitted on the Isle of Wight.

It was the class's proven ability to manage well a load of 60-75 tons (say, two bogie coaches, three at a pinch) which made them so popular with the operators of minor railways. The careers of the 'Terriers' in minor railway hands shows that however good the design, they were just as susceptible to abuse and ill-treatment as other locomotives. The Isle of Wight Central for instance had a spate of crank-axle failures, an event almost unknown on the LBSC. It suggests that the engines were either routinely overloaded or badly driven; other problems at the time suggest that maintenance at Newport was nothing to write home about. Probably the answer is that the Central, having squeezed its budget to buy the engines, felt constrained to get the last drop of blood out of them before the rash extravagance of spending money on maintenance. The condition of the Col Stephens engines also slithered inexorably downhill until by the 1930s the derelict 'Terrier' hulks in Rolvenden yard nearly reached tourist attraction status — proof that no matter how good a machine is, it will still wear out if you do not look after it.

Work on the expiring Kent & East Sussex and the impossibility of finding anything else to work the Hayling Island line kept the 'Terriers' working into the BR era, although by the mid-1950s it was clear that the class was hanging on by its finger-nails. They did gain a little status as the oldest engines on BR, which was to be useful later. The Langstone Bridge saved the last few from the carnage of 1961/62, when almost every pre-Grouping class was withdrawn in an accountancy clear-up operation when the British Transport Commission was wound up, but the decision had already been taken to close the line.

By then of course the next phase in their careers, unexpected just a few years before, was commencing. *Stepney* had become the first 'Terrier' — and the first ex-BR engine — to enter active preservation, sold to the infant Bluebell Railway and delivering itself under its own steam, with two coaches in tow, in May 1960. Even at this late date, with 11 'Terriers' still on its books, BR decided that it could not spare any more but the numbers were to trickle down until the last five were withdrawn in November 1963.

In preservation, history was to repeat itself yet again, when on the two lines where they were first active (Bluebell and KESR) they were soon outclassed by the increase in traffic. *Stepney* spent 15 years out of traffic at Bluebell from 1967, the longest period of inactivity in its career. Its eventual restoration was spurred largely by the interest of young visitors in view of its fictionalised starring role in one of the Rev Awdry's 'Railway Series' books. However, since then changes in visitor habits and shifts in policy on both lines mean that new niches have appeared for the small engines. At Bluebell they run small trains at what would be otherwise uneconomic times of the year and at the KESR the operation of the 'Vintage Train' together with a timetable veering towards more frequent but shorter trains has ensured that they have a continuing role — sufficiently so for the railway to offer a home to a third member of the class and to buy a new boiler for *Bodiam*. On neither line are they front-line locomotives and the time taken to overhaul one reflects this but they clearly have secure and useful futures as operating machines. On the Isle of Wight Steam Railway the lighter traffic, the historic significance of the engines and the small locomotive fleet mean that the 'Terriers' have a vital role to play and are liable to be busier than their sisters on the mainland.

For the 'Terriers' the wheel has turned full circle — not once but several times. Designed for working London suburban services in mid-Victorian times, seven of the class remain active and appreciated in the rural south of England and three others are valued museum exhibits — one of them, like *Brighton* so long ago, representing her country's railways overseas. William Stroudley would be absolutely delighted.

Below:
'Terriers' remain front-line motive power on the Isle of Wight Steam Railway. Hauling a substantial train of two bogies and four four-wheelers, *Freshwater* tackles the climb from Smallbrook Junction to Ashey in September 1998. *Stuart Duddy*